Apple TV®

PORTABLE GENIUS

Apple TV®

PORTABLE GENIUS

by Guy Hart-Davis

WILEY

John Wiley & Sons, Inc.

Apple TV® Portable Genius

Published by
John Wiley & Sons, Inc.
10475 Crosspoint Blvd.
Indianapolis, IN 46256
www.wiley.com

ISBN: 978-1-118-52933-1

Manufactured in the United States of America

10 9 8 7 6 5 4 3 2 1

Library of Congress Control Number: 2012954231

WILEY

Credits

Acquisitions Editor
Aaron Black

Project Editor
Amanda Gambill

Technical Editor
Paul Sihvonen-Binder

Copy Editor
Lauren Kennedy

Editorial Director
Robyn Siesky

Business Manager
Amy Knies

Senior Marketing Manager
Sandy Smith

Vice President and Executive Group Publisher
Richard Swadley

Vice President and Executive Publisher
Barry Pruett

Senior Project Coordinator
Kristie Rees

Graphics and Production Specialists
Jennifer Henry
Andrea Hornberger

Quality Control Technician
Lauren Mandelbaum

Proofreading and Indexing
Lisa Young Stiers
Potomac Indexing, LLC

About the Author

Guy Hart-Davis is the author of more than 80 computer books, including *Teach Yourself VISUALLY Mac Mini*, *Teach Yourself VISUALLY iPhone 5*, *Teach Yourself VISUALLY iMac*, and *iMac Portable Genius*.

Acknowledgments

My thanks go to the following people for making this book happen:

- Aaron Black for asking me to write this edition of the book.
- Amanda Gambill for shaping the outline and running the editorial side of the project.
- Paul Sihvonen-Binder for reviewing the book for technical accuracy and making many helpful suggestions.
- Lauren Kennedy for copyediting the book with a light touch.
- Jennifer Henry and Andrea Hornberger for laying out the book in the design.
- Lisa Young Stiers for scrutinizing the pages for errors.
- Potomac Indexing, LLC for creating the index.

Contents

Acknowledgments   ix

Introduction   xviii

---

chapter 1

How Do I Connect and
Set Up My Apple TV?   2

Unboxing Your Apple TV   4

Getting the Correct Cables and Adapters   4

   Using an HDMI cable for an HDTV   6

   Using a component or composite
   video converter   7

Connecting Your Apple TV   9

   Identifying the ports on your Apple TV   10

   Connecting your Apple TV to a TV
   or monitor   11

   Connecting your Apple TV to speakers   12

   Connecting your Apple TV to
   the Internet   13

   Connecting your Apple TV to a
   power socket   13

Setting Up Your Apple TV   13

   Starting your Apple TV and
   choosing the language   14

   Connecting your Apple TV to
   a network   14

   Choosing whether to send
   information to Apple   17

Changing the Apple TV
Internet Connection   18

   Switching from one wireless
   network to another   18

   Sharing your computer's Internet
   connection with the Apple TV   20

Putting Your Apple TV to Sleep
and Waking It   26

How Can I Customize My Apple TV? 28

How Can I Make the Most of Music on My Apple TV? 58

Naming Your Apple TV 30
Manually Configuring Network Settings 31
Testing the Network Configuration 36
Using Parental Controls 37
Pairing the Apple Remote 41
Choosing When Your Apple TV Sleeps 42
Configuring General Settings 42
    Setting the time zone 42
    Setting the language 44
    Choosing Accessibility settings 44
    Configuring Your iTunes
        Store account 45
    Choosing a screen saver 47
Choosing Audio and Video Settings 51
Setting Up AirPlay 55
Turning On Home Sharing 56

Playing Music on Your Apple TV 60
Creating a Music Library on Your
    Mac or PC 60
    Setting iTunes to create high-quality
        audio files from a CD 61
    Picking the best encoding for
        your needs 63
    Choosing where to store your library 64
    Importing a CD 66
    Adding existing music files to iTunes 69
    Converting music file formats 71
    Creating fixed playlists and
        Smart playlists 72
Playing Music from iCloud 77
    Setting up iTunes Match on
        your Mac or PC 77
    Playing music from iCloud 79
Streaming Music to Your Apple TV 86
    Streaming music from your Mac or PC 86
    Streaming music from your iOS device 87
Streaming the Screen of an iOS
    Device to Your Apple TV 88

chapter 4

How Do I Set Up and Use
Home Sharing?   90

Understanding Home Sharing	92
Setting Up Home Sharing	92
Setting up Home Sharing in iTunes	92
Setting up Home Sharing on an iOS device	96
Setting up Home Sharing on your iPad	96
Setting up Home Sharing on your iPhone or iPod touch	96
Setting up Home Sharing on your Apple TV	97
Playing Content via Home Sharing	98
Playing content via Home Sharing on another computer	98
Copying files from one computer library to another	99
Playing content via Home Sharing on Apple TV	101
Playing content via Home Sharing on an iOS device	103
Playing content via Home Sharing on an iPhone or iPod touch	103
Playing content via Home Sharing on an iPad	104

chapter 5

How Can I Watch Movies and
Videos on My Apple TV?   106

Choosing How to Watch Movies and Videos	108
Using the Movies App	109
Previewing and renting movies	112
Buying a movie	112
Searching for movies or finding them with Genius	113
Creating a Wish List and using the Purchased list	114
Using the TV Shows App	114
Browsing and Finding TV Shows	115
Viewing show information and finding episodes	117
Watching previews and adding shows to Favorites	118
Returning to previously purchased TV shows	119
Using the Trailers App	119
Watching Movies and TV Shows on Netflix	121
Selecting movies and shows	121
Viewing information about or watching a video	123
Watching Videos on Hulu Plus	123
Choosing movies and shows	124
Viewing information about and playing a video	127

Watching Videos on Vimeo 127

Launching the Vimeo app and
signing in 128

Browsing for content 128

Searching for and playing videos 130

chapter 6

How Can I Create Videos to
Watch on My Apple TV? 132

Understanding Which Video Formats
Your Apple TV Can Play 134

Checking Whether a Video Will Play
on Your Apple TV 134

Creating Videos with Your iOS Device 136

Creating Files from Video Clips on
a Mac or PC 136

Converting Video File Formats 137

Creating Video Files from DVDs 140

Understanding the legalities
of copying DVDs 140

OS X tools for copying DVD files 140

Windows tools for copying DVD files 142

chapter 7

How Can I Listen to the Radio
and Podcasts on My Apple TV? 144

Listening to the Radio 146

Opening the Radio app and
finding stations 146

Creating a list of favorite
radio stations 147

Playing an unlisted station 148

Listening to Podcasts 150

Finding podcasts 150

Viewing information about
or playing a podcast 153

Finding unlisted podcasts 154

chapter 8

What Can I Do with Photos on
My Apple TV? 156

Understanding Photo Stream 158

Setting Up Photo Stream 158

   Setting up Photo Stream on a Mac 158

   Setting up Photo Stream on a PC 160

   Setting up Photo Stream on your
     iOS device 164

   Setting up Photo Stream on
     your Apple TV 164

Viewing Photos with Photo Stream 166

   Browsing individual photos 166

   Viewing a slide show 167

   Choosing slide show settings 167

   Deleting a photo from Photo Stream 169

Browsing Photos on Flickr 169

   Adding a Flickr contact 170

      Adding a contact by name 170

      Searching for a contact 171

   Browsing a contact's albums
     and viewing slide shows 172

Using a Different Remote Control
  with Your Apple TV 176

   Choosing a suitable remote for
     the Apple TV 177

   Configuring a remote for use
     with the Apple TV 177

   Renaming, reconfiguring, or
     deleting a remote 181

Using an iOS Device as a Remote Control 183

   Downloading and installing the
     Remote app using an iOS device 183

   Downloading and installing the
     Remote app using iTunes 183

   Controlling the Apple TV with the
     Remote app 184

chapter 9

How Do I Set Up and Use
a Remote Control? 174

Replacing the Battery in the Apple
  Remote Control 176

chapter 10

What Can I Do with the
WSJ Live App? 188

Opening the WSJ Live App 190

Watching Live Broadcasts 190

Finding Programs 190

   Browsing the schedule 190

   Browsing the full list 192

   Browsing by category 194

   Searching for programs 196

chapter 11

How Can I Add More Capabilities to My Apple TV?   198

Sending Movies to Your Apple TV   200

Mirroring Your Computer on Your
Apple TV with AirParrot   202

Working with AirParrot on a Mac   202

Working with AirParrot on a PC   203

Displaying your desktop on
your Apple TV   204

Displaying a single app on
your Apple TV   205

Extending a Mac desktop to
your Apple TV   205

Understanding Jailbreaking   206

Adding Capabilities with aTV Flash   207

chapter 12

How Can I Troubleshoot My Apple TV?   210

Keeping Your Apple TV Updated   212

Performing Essential
Troubleshooting Moves   213

Restarting your Apple TV   214

Resetting your Apple TV   214

Restoring your Apple TV   215

Troubleshooting Remote Control Issues   218

The Apple Remote controls your
Mac instead of your Apple TV   218

Your Apple TV doesn't respond
to the Apple Remote   219

Checking the Apple Remote battery   220

Troubleshooting Network
and Internet Issues   220

Manually configuring the Apple TV
network settings   221

Fixing incorrect network settings   223

Troubleshooting wired network
connection issues   224

Troubleshooting wireless network
connection issues   225

The Apple TV loses its wireless
connection   225

The Apple TV has a wireless
connection but no Internet
connection   226

The Apple TV claims the
Wi-Fi password is incorrect   227

Troubleshooting Internet
connection issues   228

Your Apple TV loses its
Internet connection   228

You get a message that the
iTunes Store is unavailable   229

Troubleshooting Display Issues   230

No video appears on the TV screen   230

Video playback is choppy
or interrupted   231

App icons disappear from
the Home screen   231

Troubleshooting Home Sharing Issues   232

  Providing the conditions Home
    Sharing needs   233

    Updating to the latest
      version of iTunes   233

    Updating your iOS devices   233

    Checking your Internet
      connection   234

    Checking for other
      network issues   234

    Using the same Apple ID on
      each computer and device   235

  Troubleshooting authorization
    problems   235

  Troubleshooting connection issues   236

    Restarting iTunes   236

    Restarting your computer   237

    Restarting Home Sharing   237

    Turning on the wake for network
      access feature on a Mac   237

Troubleshooting Content Issues   239

  The Movies and TV Shows apps don't
    appear on the Home screen   239

  The Apple TV says it's not authorized
    to play content   240

  Your Apple TV gives you an
    HDCP error   240

  The Apple TV can't play content
    from the iTunes Store   241

Troubleshooting AirPlay Issues   241

  The AirPlay icon is missing from
    iTunes or your iOS device   242

  AirPlay playback is disrupted   246

    Connect your Apple TV
      via Ethernet   246

    Turn off Bluetooth on your
      iOS device   246

    Minimize interference on your
      wireless network   246

    Setting your router to give
      AirPlay higher Quality of
      Service priority   251

Configuring an Apple TV Using
Apple Configurator   252

  Getting started with Apple
    Configurator   253

  Creating a configuration profile   254

  Installing a configuration profile
    on an Apple TV   256

Index   258

Introduction

Your Apple TV is a great way to enjoy movies, videos, and TV shows — but it also offers far more than that. Its streamlined operating system and minimalist controls belie a full-powered entertainment device.

This book shows you how to get the very most out of your Apple TV. Here's just a taste of the topics that are covered:

- **Connecting your Apple TV, setting it up, and getting started.** The Apple TV is easy to set up — provided you're using the latest technology, such as HDMI (High-Definition Multimedia Interface) connections and speakers with optical inputs. However, if you're using older hardware, such as Component Video connections and analog speakers, you have to get the right equipment. Either way, you must connect your Apple TV to a wired or wireless network so that it can access the Internet.

- **Configuring your Apple TV to work the way that you prefer.** By digging into the Settings app, you can take control of everything from the device's name to the powerful AirPlay and Home Sharing features. You can also apply parental controls to protect young eyes from adult content, set up an attractive screen saver, and customize your audio and video settings.

- **Streaming music via your Apple TV.** You can use the Apple TV to stream music from your iTunes library. You can also use AirPlay to stream music to the Apple TV from your computer, iPhone, iPad, or iPod touch. To make the most of the music features, you should build a full music library in iTunes by importing your CDs and adding your existing digital audio files.

- **Sharing music and videos with Home Sharing.** By setting up Apple's innovative Home Sharing feature, you can share your music and videos among your computer, iOS devices, and Apple TV.

- **Watching movies, videos, TV shows, and trailers.** Your Apple TV gives you access to a wide range of video options, from pay content, such as the iTunes Store, Netflix, and Hulu Plus, to free videos on Vimeo.

- **Watching your own videos and DVDs on your Apple TV.** The Apple TV is designed primarily for viewing professionally produced content. However, you can also create suitable content from your own videos and DVDs.

- **Listening to Internet radio and podcasts.** With your Apple TV, you can access a huge variety of Internet radio stations, and catch up on the latest news, views, and music. You can also watch video podcasts or tune into audio podcasts.

- **Viewing photos.** Setting up Photo Stream allows you to browse photos from your computers or iOS devices on the big screen connected to your Apple TV. You can also view other people's photos on Flickr, or play photo slide shows.

- **Controlling your Apple TV with a different remote.** The Apple Remote is sleek, slim, and too small for many hands, so you may want to set up a different remote to control your Apple TV. A different remote can also provide you with extra buttons for controlling playback. You can even turn your iPhone, iPod touch, or iPad into a handy remote for your Apple TV.

- **Keeping up with financial news.** Your Apple TV includes the WSJ Live app, which gives you access to video content from the *Wall Street Journal*. You can catch up with live programming, as well as dig into the archives to research topics.

- **Adding extra capabilities.** To make the most of your Apple TV, you can add extra software to it to do things like play DVDs, stream media from devices Apple doesn't support, or browse the Web.

- **Troubleshooting.** I cover essential troubleshooting moves to resolve the problems your Apple TV is most likely to suffer, as well as specialized techniques for dealing with network issues, and ways to quash Home Sharing and content problems.

How Do I Connect and Set Up My Apple TV?

If you've just gotten your Apple TV, it's time to get it working. Your first step is to unbox it and get any extra hardware that you need, such as cables, adapters, or video converters. You are then ready to connect the Apple TV to your hardware — your TV, speakers, and Internet connection — and power it on. After that, you need to set up the Apple TV software for the first time and learn to navigate its user interface with the Apple Remote. Finally, you need to discover how to put your Apple TV to sleep and wake it again.

Unboxing Your Apple TV.. 4

Getting the Correct Cables and Adapters............................ 4

Connecting Your Apple TV 9

Setting Up Your Apple TV 13

Changing the Apple TV Internet Connection......................... 18

Putting Your Apple TV to Sleep and Waking It 26

Unboxing Your Apple TV

If you haven't already taken your Apple TV out of its box, do so now. You find the following three components:

- **Apple TV.** This is a flat box about the size of the palm of a large hand.

- **Apple Remote.** The sleek remote control, shown in Figure 1.1, is made of brushed aluminum. You use it to set up and control the Apple TV.

- **AC power cable.** The Apple TV has a standard power cable rather than a wall wart–style power supply.

Getting the Correct Cables and Adapters

The Apple TV doesn't include a cable for connecting it to your TV, so you need to get a cable unless you already have a suitable one. Similarly, you need a cable if you want to connect your Apple TV to speakers or a stereo. If your speakers or stereo are analog instead of digital, you need a digital-to-analog converter, as well. If you want to connect your Apple TV to a wired rather than a wireless network, you need an Ethernet cable. The rest of this section covers what you need to get your Apple TV connected.

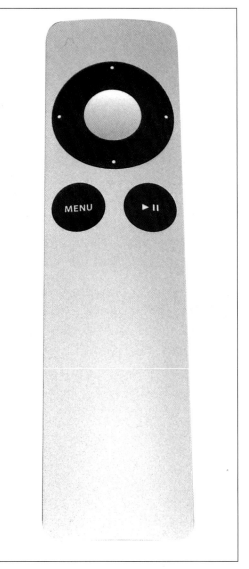

1.1 The seven buttons on the Apple Remote give you total control of your Apple TV.

At this writing, the Apple TV comes with only an High-Definition Multimedia Interface (HDMI) port for output. This is great for new and newish TVs that have one or more HDMI ports. However, if you have an older TV that doesn't have an HDMI port, you need to get a converter cable or adapter. Take a few minutes to look at your TV's documentation to find out which connections it supports. If you can't find the documentation, look at the TV itself. Figure 1.2 shows the four main types of connection: HDMI, Component Video, Composite Video, and SCART.

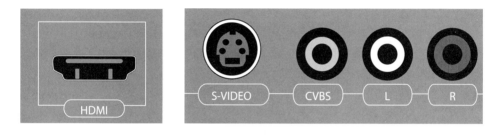

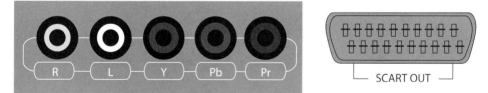

1.2 Most TVs offer one or more of these types of connections (top left to bottom right): HDMI, Component Video, Composite Video, and SCART.

Using an HDMI cable for an HDTV

For an HDTV, you normally need only an HDMI cable. If you already have a suitable HDMI cable, you're all set. If not, you can pick one up from most any store that carries electrical goods.

When you're choosing an HDMI cable, consider the following:

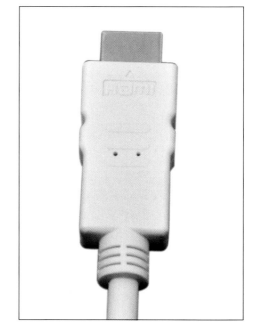

1.3 The HDMI logo indicates that the HDMI Organization has tested and approved the cable.

- **HDMI logo.** Make sure that the cable carries the HDMI logo, as shown in Figure 1.3. This means that the cable was tested and approved by the HDMI Organization — the body responsible for setting and maintaining the HDMI standard. HDMI–approved cables cost a few dollars more than those that are unapproved, but you can be confident that they are of acceptable quality.

- **Length.** If you can position your Apple TV near your TV, a three- or six-foot cable may be long enough. If the Apple TV needs to be farther away — for example, so that you can easily connect it to your wired or wireless network — get a longer cable. Extremely long cables can cause signal problems (see the sidebar about HDMI cable length), so don't buy one that is longer than you actually need.

- **Cost.** Expect to pay between $10 and $20 for a quality HDMI cable of standard length (3 to 10 feet). Audiovisual specialists make and sell extremely expensive HDMI cables, and some cost thousands of dollars. Current expert opinion, though, is that basic HDMI cables are fine as long as they are properly made and you don't mistreat them.

Caution

Avoid flat HDMI cables. Even though these can both look more stylish and be easier to run under carpets or through obstructions, they are more likely to suffer from interference than round cables. This is because an HDMI cable consists of twisted pairs of wires. A flat cable has less space than a round cable, so the wires in a flat cable need to be thinner. This gives them less resistance to interference.

HDMI standards. Some manufacturers advertise their cables as being compliant with different standards, such as HDMI 1.2 and HDMI 1.3. HDMI 1.3 supports Deep Color, a feature that uses extra colors to give a richer display, automatic lip-synching, and high-resolution soundtracks, including Dolby TrueHD. At this writing, the Apple TV doesn't use these features, so you don't need HDMI 1.3 cables. If you can choose between an HDMI 1.2 or 1.3 cable, go for the 1.3 for future compatibility.

Using a component or composite video converter

If you have a standard TV rather than an HDTV, you most likely need to use a Component Video input or Composite Video input instead of an HDMI input. If your TV provides both types of connections, use Component Video, because it gives higher quality. If your TV has only one type of connection, you're stuck with that type.

How Long Can an HDMI Cable Be?

Unlike many other audio-visual specifications, the HDMI specification doesn't give a maximum length for an HDMI cable. In practice, however, the maximum effective length for an HDMI cable is about 50 feet. Beyond this length, the signal tends to lose strength, which means that your TV doesn't get a strong enough signal to produce a good picture.

If the HDMI cable is too long or damaged, you may notice the following symptoms:

- Distortion in the picture.
- Single pixels failing to appear in the correct color.
- No video at all, even though the audio plays correctly.

If you need to run the HDMI cable a long distance and find these symptoms appearing, get an HDMI signal restorer to strengthen the signal.

If your TV has a Component Video input, get an HDMI-to–Component Video converter like the one shown in Figure 1.4. This converter is a small box with an HDMI input at one end, as shown on the left in Figure 1.4, and a Component Video output at the other, as shown on the right in Figure 1.4. You also need a Component Video cable if you don't already have one.

1.4 Use an HDMI-to–Component Video converter (left) to connect your Apple TV to a standard TV via a Component Video input (right).

If your TV has a Composite Video input, you can get an HDMI-to–Composite Video converter. Similar to the Component Video converter, this is a small box with an HDMI input at one end, as shown on the left in Figure 1.5, and a Composite Video output at the other, as shown on the right in Figure 1.5. You also need a Composite Video cable to connect the converter to your TV's input.

1.5 Use an HDMI-to–Composite Video converter (left) to connect your Apple TV to a standard TV via a Composite Video input (right).

Choosing Which TV Connection to Use

If your TV has several types of connection, make sure you use the most suitable one. The following list explains the connection types in descending order of preference:

- **HDMI.** If your TV has HDMI, use it. HDMI can carry both video and audio, so you don't need a separate audio connection.

- **Component Video.** Component Video uses five cables for transferring audio and video. Two cables carry the audio: one carries the left audio channel and the other carries the right audio channel. Three cables carry the video: The first carries the red signal, the second the green signal, and the third the blue signal. Component Video provides better quality than Composite Video, so use it as your second choice if HDMI isn't available.

- **Composite Video.** Composite Video uses three cables for transferring audio and video: The first carries the left audio channel, the second carries the right audio channel, and the third carries the combined video signal. Putting all of the video on a single cable provides a lower-quality picture than using three separate cables, as Component Video does.

- **SCART.** (Also known as Péritel, EuroSCART, EuroAV, or Euroconnector.) If your TV has only SCART connections, you can buy a Component Video to SCART converter box to connect your Apple TV.

Connecting Your Apple TV

In this section, I cover how to make the physical connections to your Apple TV. First, identify the ports on the back of the Apple TV, and then connect it to your TV or monitor, speakers, and wired network (if you use one). Finally, connect the power supply.

Identifying the ports on your Apple TV

On the back of your Apple TV are the following five ports, as shown in Figure 1.6:

- **Ethernet.** Plug an Ethernet cable into this port to connect your Apple TV to a wired network.

1.6 The back of the Apple TV features an Ethernet port, an optical digital audio port, an HDMI port, a micro USB port, and a power connector.

- **Optical digital audio.** Plug an optical digital audio cable with a TOSLINK connector into this port to connect your Apple TV to digital speakers. The acronym TOSLINK comes from Toshiba Link.

- **HDMI.** Plug an HDMI cable into this port to connect your Apple TV to your TV or monitor.

- **Micro USB.** This port is for diagnosing problems and servicing the device. Normally, you don't need to connect anything to this port.

- **Power.** Plug the AC power cable into this port and connect the other end to a power socket.

Note

See Chapter 12 for instructions on using the Micro USB port to diagnose problems and reinstall older versions of iOS on your Apple TV.

If you have a wired network and a TV with an HDMI port, you should be able to connect your Apple TV in seconds by plugging in an Ethernet and HDMI cable, and the power cord.

Connecting your Apple TV to a TV or monitor

First, connect your Apple TV to the TV or monitor on which you want to display the picture. The quick and easy way to make the connection is to plug one end of an HDMI cable into the Apple TV and the other end into your TV or monitor. However, if your TV or monitor doesn't have an HDMI port, you have to convert from HDMI to a port type the TV or monitor does have. The following are the available options:

- **Connect your Apple TV to an HDTV.** To connect your Apple TV to an HDTV, you simply need an HDMI cable. Plug one end of it into the HDMI port on the Apple TV and the other end into the HDMI port on the TV, and you're in business. If your TV doesn't auto-matically detect the HDMI input, you may need to select it manually by using your remote control.

- **Connect your Apple TV to a standard TV.** To connect your Apple TV to a standard TV, you have to convert the HDMI signal to either Component Video or Composite Video, depending on the TV's inputs. Use an HDMI cable to connect the Apple TV's HDMI port to the HDMI input on the converter device. Then use a Component Video cable or a Composite Video cable to connect the device's output to the TV.

- **Connect your Apple TV to a monitor.** Instead of connecting your Apple TV to a TV, you can connect it to a monitor. If your monitor has an HDMI connection, simply connect the Apple TV using an HDMI cable. HDMI carries the audio along with the video, so you can listen to the audio on the monitor's speakers (if it has speakers) or through speakers or headphones connected to the monitor's audio output.

Genius If your monitor has a choice of inputs, choose HDMI first and DVI (digital video inter-face) second. Use VGA only if you have no other choice.

If your monitor has a DVI input, get a cable that converts from HDMI to DVI. Similarly, if your moni-tor has a VGA input, buy a cable that converts from HDMI to VGA.

Note The VGA connector is also called a D-sub connector.

Connecting your Apple TV to speakers

You can play audio from your Apple TV through a TV or the speakers connected to it. However, if you prefer, you can also connect your Apple TV directly to your speakers — or to headphones if those are more convenient. If you have digital speakers, connect an optical audio cable to the audio out port on the back of the Apple TV and to the audio input on the speakers. Optical audio cables are also called TOSLINK cables and they come in various lengths up to around 30 feet.

Note Beyond about 15 or 20 feet, optical audio cables tend to suffer from attenuation (that is, loss of signal). If you need a longer cable, make sure that you get a high-quality one. All other things being equal, multi-strand cables provide better performance than single-strand.

If you have analog speakers, you have to convert the Apple TV's digital output to an analog signal. To do so, you need to get a digital-to-analog (DAC) converter like the one shown in Figure 1.7. It consists of a small box with an optical input at one end (shown on the left in Figure 1.7) and an analog output at the other (shown on the right in Figure 1.7). You can get these from any decent electronics store and from many sources online, including Amazon and eBay. As usual, it's a good idea to either test the device in person or read a selection of reviews before you make your purchase.

1.7 Use a digital-to-analog converter to convert the Apple TV's digital output to an analog signal for analog speakers.

Caution Avoid bending an optical audio cable tightly when routing it around your home or stereo. Bending the cable can cause it either to fail temporarily (until you straighten it) or to break permanently.

Connecting your Apple TV to the Internet

To stream content such as videos or your music from iCloud, your Apple TV needs an Internet connection. To connect the Apple TV to the Internet, you simply connect it to either a wired or wireless network that is already connected to the Internet.

Genius
If you have both a wired and wireless network, connect your Apple TV to the wired network for greater speed and stability. Even though wireless networks have improved immeasurably since the turn of the millennium, wired networks remain faster and more reliable.

To connect your Apple TV to a wired network, simply connect an Ethernet cable from the network's router or switch to the Ethernet port on the back of the Apple TV. To connect your Apple TV to a wireless network, make sure you know the network's name and security information — for example, the password. You then choose the network and provide the security information after starting the Apple TV.

Note
If your Internet router is directly connected to your PC or Mac rather than to a network switch or wireless access point, you can share the Internet connection from your computer by using Internet Connection Sharing (ICS) on Windows or Internet Sharing on the Mac. I explain how to do this later in this chapter.

Connecting your Apple TV to a power socket

The final step is to connect the Apple TV AC power cable to the device's power input and a power socket. You can simply connect the AC power cable directly to a socket, but it's a good idea to use a surge protector or uninterruptible power supply to protect the Apple TV against spikes and brownouts in the power supply. An uninterruptible power supply also ensures that the Apple TV doesn't lose power if there's a power outage.

Setting Up Your Apple TV

After making the physical connections, you're ready to set up your Apple TV's software. In this section, I show you how to start your Apple TV, choose the language for the user interface, and connect to your wireless network (if necessary).

Starting your Apple TV and choosing the language

To start your Apple TV, press any button on the Apple Remote. You'll see the white status light on the right side of the Apple TV's front face come on. After a few seconds, the Welcome to Apple TV screen appears. Highlight your language by pressing the Up or Down buttons on the Apple Remote, and then press the Select button to select the language.

Connecting your Apple TV to a network

What your Apple TV needs next is a wired or wireless network connection that gives it access to your Internet connection. If you've plugged in an Ethernet cable, your Apple TV automatically attempts to connect to the Internet. If it can do so, it contacts the Apple servers and requests activation.

Using the Apple Remote to Navigate the Apple TV

See the following list to navigate using the Apple Remote:

- **Up, Down, Left, and Right buttons.** Press one of these to highlight the next item in that particular direction. For example, press the Right button to highlight the item to the right of the one that is highlighted.

- **Select button.** Press this button (the one in the center of the remote) to choose the item that is currently highlighted.

- **Menu button.** Press this button to go up one level in the Apple TV menu structure. The Home screen is the top level of the menu, so you can't go any farther from there.

- **Play/Pause button.** Pressing the Play/Pause button starts playback. Pressing it again pauses playback and pressing it a third time resumes playback.

To choose an item, use the Up, Down, Left, and Right buttons to move the blue highlight to it, and then press the Select button. Going forward, this book refers to choosing an item this way as *selecting*.

Note If your network router uses Dynamic Host Configuration Protocol (DHCP) to assign IP addresses to network devices, your Apple TV automatically requests an IP address when you start it. Most network routers use DHCP, but if yours doesn't, you can assign your Apple TV an IP address manually, as described later in this chapter.

If no cable is connected to its Ethernet port, your Apple TV displays the first Wi-Fi Network screen. This screen shows the list of wireless networks the Apple TV has detected.

Genius If the wireless network to which you want to connect doesn't appear in the list of wireless networks, press the Menu button to return to the Network screen, and then select Configure Wi-Fi. This forces your Apple TV to scan for wireless networks again. If the network still doesn't appear, select Other, and then type the network name.

Follow these steps to connect the Apple TV to your wireless network:

1. **Select the wireless network to which you want to connect the Apple TV, as shown in Figure 1.8.** If the wireless network doesn't appear in the list on the Wi-Fi Network screen, perform the following actions:

   - **Select Other.** Another Wi-Fi Network screen appears.

Wi-Fi Network

To connect to the Internet, choose your Wi-Fi network, or connect using an ethernet cable. If you don't see your Wi-Fi network, select Other.

AirPort Express

HD

HD 5GHz

Surreal Macs AP

Surreal Macs AP01

Surreal Macs AP02

Surreal Macs AP03

Other...

1.8 On the first Wi-Fi Network screen, select your wireless network. If it doesn't appear in the list, select Other.

● **Enter the network name, as shown in Figure 1.9, and then select Submit.** If the Wi-Fi Password screen doesn't appear, the wireless network has no password, and you can skip steps 2 and 3.

Wi-Fi Network

abc   ABC   #+=   Recent

Enter the name of the network you want to join and then select Submit.

a	b	c	d	e	f
g	h	i	j	k	l
m	n	o	p	q	r
s	t	u	v	w	x
y	z	1	2	3	4
5	6	7	8	9	0

Network:

HighWire

. _ @ .com .net .edu

SPACE   DELETE   CLEAR

Submit

Press ► II to change keyboards

1.9 To join a closed wireless network (one that doesn't broadcast its name), enter its name on the Wi-Fi Network screen.

2. **On the Wi-Fi Password screen shown in Figure 1.10, use the on-screen keyboard in the following ways to type the password:**

   ● **Press the Up, Down, Left, or Right buttons to highlight the character that you want to type, and then press the Select button to type it.**

   ● **Press the Play/Pause button one or more times to cycle through the available keyboards, which are abc (lowercase letters), ABC (uppercase letters), #+= (sym- bols and accented letters), and Recent (items, if any, that you've typed recently).** You can also change keyboards by highlighting the one that you want, and then pressing the Select button.

   ● **Highlight Delete, and then press the Select button to delete the previous character.**

   ● **Highlight Clear, and then press the Select button to clear all characters.**

3. **Select Submit.** You see the Connecting screen as your Apple TV tries to establish the connection, and then the Activating screen if it succeeds.

1.10 On the Wi-Fi Password screen, type the wireless network's password using the on-screen keyboard.

Choosing whether to send information to Apple

After your Apple TV has connected to the Internet, it displays a screen asking permission to auto-matically send Apple information about how you use it and how it's working. Select OK or No Thanks, as appropriate. Once you've performed the initial setup routine, the Apple TV Home screen appears, as shown in Figure 1.11.

1.11 When the Home screen appears, you can start navigating with the Apple Remote.

Changing the Apple TV Internet Connection

As covered earlier in this chapter, you can usually set up the Apple TV Internet connection rather easily. After the initial setup, though, you may need to switch from a wired network to a wireless one, a wireless network to a wired one, or from one wireless network to another. You may also need to connect your Apple TV to the Internet through an Internet connection connected directly to your Mac or PC. This type of connection can be useful both at home and when you travel.

Note When you connect your Apple TV to a network, it normally acquires an IP address and other network settings automatically via DHCP. However, if the network doesn't use DHCP, you need to choose network settings manually. See Chapter 2 for instructions.

If you normally connect your Apple TV to a wired network, you can easily switch it to a wireless network. To do so, unplug the Ethernet cable from your Apple TV, and then follow the procedure explained earlier in this chapter.

Note You cannot connect your Apple TV to a wireless network without unplugging the Ethernet cable from it (or unplugging the other end of the Ethernet cable from the switch, hub, or router). This is because the Apple TV uses the Ethernet connection in preference to a wireless connection.

To switch your Apple TV from a wireless network to a wired network, simply plug the network cable back into the Ethernet port on the Apple TV. The Apple TV then establishes a connection across the Ethernet cable.

Switching from one wireless network to another

Follow these steps to change the wireless network your Apple TV is using:

1. **Press the Menu button one or more times, as needed, to display the Home screen.**

2. **Choose Settings ⇨ General ⇨ Network.** The Network screen appears.

3. **Select Configure Wi-Fi, as shown in Figure 1.12.** The first Wi-Fi Network screen appears, showing the list of available wireless networks.

4. **Select the wireless network you want to use.** The Wi-Fi Password screen appears.

5. **Enter the password.**

6. **Select Submit.** The Apple TV attempts to connect to the wireless network. The Configuration Succeeded screen, shown in Figure 1.13, appears when the connection is made.

7. **Select Done.** The Apple TV displays the network's name, the IP and Wi-Fi addresses, and the signal strength, as shown in Figure 1.14.

8. **Press the Menu button to return to the General screen.**

Network

Configure Wi-Fi	❯
Configure TCP/IP	›
Test Network	›

Network Name	HD 5GHz
IP Address	DHCP 10.0.0.37
Subnet Mask	255.255.255.0
Router Address	10.0.0.2
DNS Address	10.0.0.2
Wi-Fi Address	58:55:ca:0d:36:57
Signal Strength	▪▪▪▪▪

1.12 On the Network screen, select Configure Wi-Fi to start connecting Apple TV to a wireless network.

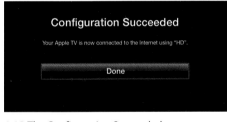

Configuration Succeeded

Your Apple TV is now connected to the Internet using "HD".

Done

1.13 The Configuration Succeeded screen confirms that your Apple TV is connected to the wireless network.

Network

Configure Wi-Fi	❯
Configure TCP/IP	›
Test Network	›

Network Name	HD
IP Address	DHCP 10.0.0.37
Subnet Mask	255.255.255.0
Router Address	10.0.0.2
DNS Address	10.0.0.2
Wi-Fi Address	58:55:ca:0d:36:57
Signal Strength	▪▪▪▪▪

1.14 The Details screen displays all necessary information about the wireless network.

Genius

The Wi-Fi address is the hardware address of the Apple TV's Wi-Fi adapter. This address is also called the Media Access Control address, or MAC address for short. You may need this to add the Wi-Fi to a network that uses a white list of MAC addresses. The white list permits only authorized computers and devices to join the network.

Sharing your computer's Internet connection with the Apple TV

If your Internet connection is connected to your Mac or PC instead of to a network switch or wireless access point, you may need to share the Internet connection using the Mac or PC rather than using hardware. You can do this by using the Internet Sharing feature on the Mac or the Internet Connection Sharing (ICS) feature on Windows.

Note

The OS X Internet Sharing feature is great for situations in which you can't share an Internet connection via the network using a router or switch, such as when you're in a dorm or hotel room with a single Ethernet connection. However, you can't put your Mac to sleep (let alone turn it off) without cutting off the Internet connection for your Apple TV, and any other computers or devices on the network.

Follow these steps to share a Mac's Internet connection via Internet Sharing:

1. **Choose one of the following ways to share the connection:**

   * **Ethernet.** Choose this option if your Mac's Ethernet port is free. For example, if your Internet router connects to your Mac via USB instead of Ethernet, you can use this option.

   * **Wi-Fi.** Choose this option if your Mac's Ethernet port is busy or if it doesn't have a built-in Ethernet port.

2. **If you're using Ethernet, connect a cable from your Mac's Ethernet port to your Apple TV's Ethernet port.**

3. **Choose Apple menu ⇨ System Preferences.** The System Preferences window opens.

4. **In the Internet & Wireless section, click the Sharing icon to open Sharing preferences.**

5. **In the list box on the left, click Internet Sharing to display its options.** Don't select the check box just yet; simply click the Internet Sharing item in the Service column, as shown in Figure 1.15.

1.15 Internet Sharing lets you quickly share your Mac's Internet connection with your Apple TV, as well as other computers and devices on the network.

6. **In the Share your connection from pop-up menu, choose the Internet connection you want to share.** In Figure 1.15, the Internet connection is connected via USB.

7. **In the To computers using box, select the check box for each connection type you want to use.** Normally, your choices are Ethernet, FireWire, and Wi-Fi. You want to use either Ethernet or Wi-Fi to share with your Apple TV.

8. **If you selected the Wi-Fi check box, click Wi-Fi Options to open the Configure an internet-sharing network dialog, as shown in Figure 1.16.** Perform the following to set up the wireless network:

   ● **Type the name for the network in the Network Name box.**

1.16 When you use Internet Sharing via Wi-Fi, set up a wireless network in the Configure an internet-sharing network dialog.

   ● **In the Security pop-up menu, choose WPA2 Personal.**

   ● **Type a password in the Password and Confirm Password boxes.**

   ● **Click OK.** The Configure an internet-sharing network dialog closes, returning you to Sharing preferences.

9. **Select the Internet Sharing option from the list box on the left.** OS X displays a confirmation message warning you that turning on Internet Sharing may disrupt the network.

10. **Click Start to start Internet Connection sharing.**

Your Apple TV now accesses your Internet connection in one of the following ways, depending on which you chose:

- **Ethernet.** Your Apple TV automatically establishes a network connection.

- **Wi-Fi.** You connect to the wireless network you just created using the connection techniques discussed earlier in this chapter.

Here's how to share your Internet connection via ICS in Windows:

1. **Choose Start ➪ Control Panel.** An Explorer window opens showing Control Panel.

2. **In the View by drop-down list, choose Large icons, as shown in Figure 1.17.** Control Panel then displays its contents as large icons (see Figure 1.18).

1.17 In the Control Panel window, choose Large Icons to display the applets as icons.

Note This example uses Windows 7, but the procedure for Windows 8 is almost exactly the same.

1.18 Control Panel in the Large Icons view.

3. **Click Network and Sharing Center.** The Control Panel window displays the Network and Sharing Center, as shown in Figure 1.19.

1.19 In the Network and Sharing Center window, click Change adapter settings.

4. **In the left column, click Change adapter settings.** The Network Connections screen appears.

5. **Right-click the network connection that is connected to the Internet, and then click Properties on the context menu, as shown in Figure 1.20.** The Properties dialog box for the connection opens.

1.20 Click Properties on the context menu to display the connection's Properties dialog box.

6. **Click the Sharing tab to display its contents.**

7. **Select the Allow other network users to connect through this computer's Internet connection check box, as shown in Figure 1.21.**

8. **Select the Allow other network users to control or disable the shared Internet connection check box if you want other computers to be able to start the network connection or shut it down.** If your Internet connection isn't permanently connected, this is usually a good idea. If your Internet connection is permanently connected, you may prefer to deselect this check box.

Local Area Connection Properties

Networking | Sharing

Internet Connection Sharing

☑ Allow other network users to connect through this computer's Internet connection

☑ Allow other network users to control or disable the shared Internet connection

Using ICS (Internet Connection Sharing)   [Settings...]

[OK]   [Cancel]

1.21 On the Sharing tab, select the Allow other network users to connect through this computer's Internet connection check box.

9. **Click OK.** The Properties dialog box closes, and Windows applies the sharing option you chose to the Internet connection.

You can now connect your Apple TV to the same network as your PC, either via Ethernet or Wi-Fi, and the Apple TV can share the PC's Internet connection.

Putting Your Apple TV to Sleep and Waking It

When you finish using your Apple TV for the time being, it's a good idea to put it to sleep. To do so, choose Settings ⇨ Sleep Now, as shown in Figure 1.22. To wake your Apple TV, press any button on the remote control.

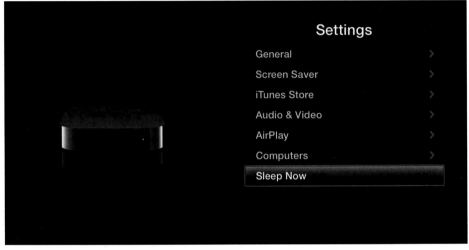

Settings

General	>
Screen Saver	>
iTunes Store	>
Audio & Video	>
AirPlay	>
Computers	>
Sleep Now	

1.22 You can put your Apple TV to sleep at any time.

Note   Your Apple TV can automatically put itself to sleep after a set period of inactivity. Normally, the Apple TV comes configured to put itself to sleep after 30 minutes. Chapter 2 shows you how to set the length of time before it goes to sleep.

How Can I Customize My Apple TV?

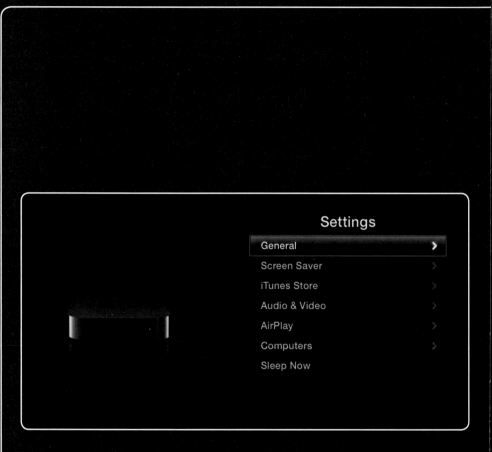

In this chapter, I explain how you can take advantage of the Apple TV's full range of settings. You can give your Apple TV a different name, change its network settings, or apply parental controls to protect young eyes from adult content. You can use other remote controls, as well as select a screen saver, and suitable audio and video settings. You can also set up your iTunes Store account, use the AirPlay feature for mirroring content, and enable the Home Sharing feature to access your music library on your computer.

Naming Your Apple TV 30

Manually Configuring Network Settings 31

Testing the Network Configuration 36

Using Parental Controls 37

Pairing the Apple Remote 41

Choosing When Your Apple TV Sleeps 42

Configuring General Settings 42

Choosing Audio and Video Settings. 51

Setting Up AirPlay 55

Turning on Home Sharing 56

Naming Your Apple TV

Your Apple TV comes with the default name "Apple TV." This works fine if you have only one Apple TV, but if you have multiple Apple TVs, or if any of your neighbors has an Apple TV within wireless range of yours, you can change the name to avoid confusion.

To change the Apple TV's name, follow these steps:

1. **Select Settings to display the Settings screen, as shown on the opening page of this chapter.**

2. **Select General to display the General screen, shown in Figure 2.1.**

3. **Select Name to display the first Name screen.**

4. **If one of the existing names is suitable, highlight it, as shown in Figure 2.2, and then press the Select button (the button in the center of the Apple Remote).** The name then appears on the General screen and you can skip the following steps. Otherwise, highlight Custom, and then press the Select button to display the second Name screen.

5. **Type the name that you want to give your Apple TV, as shown in Figure 2.3.**

6. **Select Submit.** The name appears on the General screen.

2.1 From the General screen, select Name to change your Apple TV's name.

2.2 On the first Name screen, select one of the suggested names or Custom.

Name

abc	**ABC**	#+=	Recent

Enter a name for your Apple TV

```
A   B   C   D   E   F
G   H   I   J   K   L
M   N   O   P   Q   R
S   T   U   V   W   X
Y   Z   1   2   3   4
5   6   7   8   9   0
.   _   @   .com  .net  .edu
```

SPACE   DELETE   CLEAR

Press ▶ II to change keyboards

Name

Susie's Apple TV

Submit

2.3 On the second Name screen, type a name for your Apple TV.

Manually Configuring Network Settings

If you connected your Apple TV to a wired or wireless network as covered in Chapter 1, you probably don't need to make any changes to the network configuration. However, if you are having network problems or need to configure the network in a particular way, you can manually set the subnet mask, and the IP (Internet Protocol), router, and DNS (Domain Name Service) server addresses.

Here's how to manually configure network settings:

1. **Select Settings to display the Settings screen.**
2. **Select General to display the General screen.**
3. **Select Network to display the Network screen.**

4. **Select Configure TCP/IP, as shown in Figure 2.4, to display the Network Setup screen.**

5. **Select Manually, as shown in Figure 2.5, to display the first Ethernet TCP/IP Setup screen.** Here, you can set the IP address.

Network

| Configure TCP/IP | ❯ |
| Test Network | ❯ |

IP Address	DHCP 10.0.0.37
Subnet Mask	255.255.255.0
Router Address	10.0.0.2
DNS Address	10.0.0.2
Ethernet Address	58:55:ca:0d:36:58

To switch to Wi-Fi, disconnect the Ethernet
cable from your Apple TV.

2.4 From the Network screen, select Configure TCP/IP to change your Apple TV's network settings.

Network Setup

For most networks, automatic configuration is sufficient. If you have a custom
network with specifically assigned IP addresses, choose Manually.

Configure IP: Automatically
                          Manually

2.5 On the Network Setup screen, select Manually to start configuring your
Apple TV's network settings.

Note If your Apple TV is using a wireless network, the network configuration screens are titled Wi-Fi TCP/IP Setup instead of Wi-Fi Ethernet Setup.

6. **Set the IP address that you want the Apple TV to use, as shown in Figure 2.6.** Press the Right and Left buttons to navigate to the figure that you want to change. Press the Up button to increase the number or the Down button to decrease it.

Ethernet TCP/IP Setup

Enter the IP address for your Apple TV and then select Done.

IP Address: 0 1 0 . 0 0 0 . 0 0 0 . 0 3 7 DONE

2.6 On the first Ethernet TCP/IP Setup screen, enter the IP address.

Genius

If one of the TCP/IP Setup settings is correct, you can quickly select Done by pressing the Left button. This is much faster than pressing the Right button multiple times to get to the Done button.

7. **Select Done.** Your Apple TV displays the second Ethernet TCP/IP Setup screen, on which you can set the subnet mask.

Note

A network can be broken up into a number of subdivisions called subnets. The sub-net mask is a four-part number that tells the computer which subnet to use. Most home networks use this subnet mask: 255.255.255.0.

8. **Adjust the subnet mask if necessary, as shown in Figure 2.7.**

Ethernet TCP/IP Setup

If you have a subnet mask, enter it and then select Done.

Subnet Mask: 2 5 5 . 2 5 5 . 2 5 5 . 0 0 0 DONE

2.7 On the second Ethernet TCP/IP Setup screen, specify the subnet mask.

9. **Select Done.** Your Apple TV displays the third Ethernet TCP/IP Setup screen, on which you can set the router address. The router is the network device that directs traffic around the network, such as your cable or DSL modem.

Note

10. **Change the router address if needed, as shown in Figure 2.8.**

Ethernet TCP/IP Setup

If you have a router IP address, enter it and then select Done.

Router Address: 0 1 0 . 0 0 0 . 0 0 0 . 0 0 2 DONE

2.8 On the third Ethernet TCP/IP Setup screen, enter the address of your network's router, and then select Done.

11. **Select Done.** Your Apple TV displays the fourth Ethernet TCP/IP Setup screen, on which you can set the IP address of the DNS server your Apple TV should use. The DNS server is the device that tells the computer how to resolve web addresses (such as www.google.com) to IP addresses (such as 173.194.41.70).

Note

12. **Change the DNS address if needed, as shown in Figure 2.9.**

13. **Select Done.** Your Apple TV displays the Configuration Done! screen.

14. **Select Done.** The Network screen appears again.

After manually configuring your network settings, you can start using your Apple TV again. But first you may want to test your network configuration, as described next.

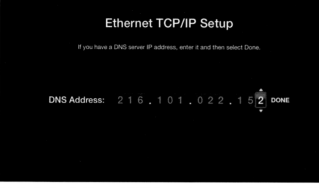

2.9 On the fourth Ethernet TCP/IP Setup screen, enter the address of the DNS server.

Connecting to the Internet through a Proxy Server

The Apple TV doesn't provide configuration settings for connecting to the Internet through a proxy server. A *proxy server* is a server that redirects Internet requests to a different source (for example, in a different country) and may also cache Internet content so that it can deliver the content more quickly.

If you need to connect your Apple TV to the Internet through a proxy server, you can run the proxy server on the Internet connection to which the Apple TV connects in one of the following ways:

- **Run a proxy server on your router.** If you use a proxy service, such as StrongVPN (www.strongvpn.com), you may be able to flash your router's firmware with software called DD-WRT (www.dd-wrt.com) to add proxying to it. Only some routers support DD-WRT, so consult your router's documentation if you need this feature. Apple's AirPort devices don't support DD-WRT.

- **Run the proxy software on your computer.** If you can't add a proxy to your router, run the proxy software on your Mac or PC. Share the Internet connection, as described in Chapter 1, and then connect your Apple TV to the shared connection.

- **Configure the Apple TV using Apple Configurator on a Mac.** Apple provides a tool called Apple Configurator for automating the configuration of iOS devices, including the Apple TV. See Chapter 12 for more details.

Testing the Network Configuration

If your Apple TV doesn't play videos smoothly, there may be a problem with the network configuration. To help Apple identify problems with streaming video, you can use the Apple TV's Network Test feature.

Genius   The Network Test feature doesn't identify or fix problems with your Apple TV's network configuration beyond giving errors if it cannot establish a connection. This feature is for providing Apple with information about video streaming conditions.

Here's how to use Network Test:

1. **From the Home screen, select Settings to display the Settings screen.**

2. **Select General to display the General screen.**

3. **Select Network to display the Network screen.**

4. **Select Test Network.** The Network Test screen appears, warning you that the test sends information to Apple to help it diagnose and improve network streaming performance.

5. **Select OK.** The iTunes Store Account screen appears.

Note   If your iTunes Store account is fully set up, your Apple TV may not prompt you for its details.

6. **Verify that your Apple ID is correct in the Apple ID field.** If not, enter the correct Apple ID.

7. **Select Submit.** If the iTunes Store Password screen prompts you for your password, enter it, and then select Submit. The first Network Test screen appears.

8. **Select Yes, as shown in Figure 2.10.** The second Network Test screen appears.

9. **Select the download speed that your Internet connection is supposed to deliver, such as 2.5 to 4 Mbps, as shown in Figure 2.11.** The download test then runs.

10. **When the final Network Test screen appears, telling you that the network test completed successfully, select Done.**

Network Test

Are you currently experiencing slow performance when streaming?

Yes

No

Cancel

2.10 On the first Network Test screen, select Yes to run the test.

Network Test

What download speed do you expect from your Internet connection?

Don't know

Faster than 10 Mbps

6 to 10 Mbps

4 to 6 Mbps

2.5 to 4 Mbps

Less than 2.5 Mbps

2.11 On the second Network Test screen, select the download speed that you expect from your Internet connection.

Using Parental Controls

If you share your Apple TV with children or other users you want to protect from accessing unsuitable content, set up parental controls. Parental controls let you do the following:

- **Choose whether features such as iTunes Match, YouTube, Internet radio, podcasts, and Netflix are available.** If you don't want any users to be able to use an item, you can hide it. If you want some users to be able to use an item, you can set the Apple TV to require a passcode to access it.

- Choose the country whose ratings scheme you want to use for movies and TV shows.

- Restrict movies and TV shows by their age ratings.

- Require a passcode to access explicit music and podcasts.

Here's how to set up parental controls:

1. **Select Settings to display the Settings screen.**

2. **Select General to display the General screen.**

3. **Select Parental Controls to display the Parental Controls screen.** When Parental Controls are turned off, the Parental Controls screen appears with most of its options dimmed and unavailable.

4. **Select Turn On Parental Controls, as shown in Figure 2.12.** The Set Passcode screen appears.

Parental Controls

Turn On Parental Controls

iTunes Match
YouTube
Internet Radio
Internet Photos
Podcasts
Trailers
Netflix
Vimeo

2.12 Select Turn On Parental Controls to start configuring parental controls.

5. **Set a four-digit passcode, as shown in Figure 2.13, to prevent unauthorized changes and allow access to restricted items.** Press the Right and Left buttons to navigate to the figure that you want to change. Press the Up button to increase the number or the Down button to decrease it.

Set Passcode

To set parental controls for your Apple TV for the first time, enter a four-digit passcode. After your passcode is set, you'll need to enter it to make changes to parental controls in the future.

2 7 2 6   DONE

2.13 On the Set Passcode screen, enter a four-digit passcode to prevent unauthorized changes to your Apple TV.

6. **Select Done.** The Confirm Passcode screen appears.

7. **Re-enter the passcode.**

Genius

If you forget your passcode, you cannot recover it. But you can reset your Apple TV to its default settings — without a passcode — by using the Reset All Settings command. See Chapter 12 for instructions.

8. **Select Done.** The Passcode Confirmed screen appears.

9. **Select OK.** The Parental Controls screen appears again, this time with all of the options enabled.

10. **Highlight iTunes Match, and then press the Select button to toggle between Show and Hide.** Show makes the iTunes Match item appear in the user interface; Hide hides this item.

11. **Highlight the YouTube, Internet Radio, Internet Photos, Podcasts, Trailers, Netflix, and Vimeo items, and then press the Select button to toggle among Ask, Show, and Hide, as needed.**

Note

The Ask setting for items such as YouTube and Netflix makes these items appear in the user interface. When someone tries to access such a feature, the Apple TV prompts for the parental controls passcode.

12. **Highlight Rental, and then press the Select button to toggle among Ask, Allow, and Hide, as needed.**

13. **Highlight Ratings For, and then press the Select button to move through the list of countries until the appropriate one appears.**

14. **Highlight Restrict Movies To, and then press the Select button to choose the rating that you want to apply.**

15. **Highlight Explicit Music & Podcasts, and then press the Select button to toggle between Ask and Allow, as needed.**

16. **Press the Menu button to return to the General screen in Settings.**

Note

When you no longer need parental controls, select Settings ⇨ General ⇨ Parental Controls, select Turn Off Parental Controls, enter the passcode, and then select Done.

Understanding the Restriction Ratings

The ratings in the Restrict Movies To and the Restrict TV Shows To lists depend on the country that you specify in the Ratings For setting. For example, if you choose United States, the Restrict Movies To setting offers these restriction choices:

- **G.** Suitable for general audiences.
- **PG.** Parental guidance suggested.
- **PG-13.** Parental guidance recommended; some material may be unsuitable for children under 13.
- **R.** Restricted. Children under 17 need an accompanying adult.

If you choose United States in the Ratings For setting, the Restrict TV Shows To setting provides these restriction options:

- **TV-Y.** Suitable for children age 2 and older.
- **TV-Y7.** Suitable for children age 7 and older.
- **TV-G.** Suitable for general audiences.
- **TV-PG.** Parental guidance suggested.
- **TV-14.** Some material may be unsuitable for children under 14.
- **TV-MA.** Suitable for mature audiences; some material may be unsuitable for children under 17.

Choose the No setting if you want to remove all restrictions from movies or TV shows.

Pairing the Apple Remote

Your Apple TV comes with an Apple Remote that's set up to work with it out of the box but isn't paired with it. *Paired* means that the Apple Remote is keyed to the Apple TV so that the Apple TV won't respond to other remotes and the Apple Remote cannot command another Apple TV. If you have only one Apple TV within range of your Apple Remote, you won't need to pair the Apple Remote with the Apple TV. However, if you have multiple Apple TVs, it's a good idea to pair each one with its Apple Remote so that you don't get your signals crossed.

To pair your Apple Remote with your Apple TV, follow these steps:

1. **Select Settings to display the Settings screen.**

2. **Select General to display the General screen.**

3. **Select Remotes to display the Remotes screen.**

4. **Select Pair Apple Remote, as shown in Figure 2.14.** The Apple TV pairs the remote and Unpair Apple Remote appears in place of the previous command.

2.14 Select Pair Apple Remote so that the Apple Remote and Apple TV communicate only with each other.

5. **Press the Menu button to return to the General screen.**

From the Remotes screen, you can also set up the Remote app on an iOS device (for example, your iPhone) or set up the Apple TV to work with another remote control. I show you how to take these actions in Chapter 9.

Choosing When Your Apple TV Sleeps

As I covered in Chapter 1, when you're not using your Apple TV, you can put it to sleep by choosing Settings ⇨ Sleep Now. However, it's usually more convenient to set your Apple TV to put itself to sleep after you haven't used it for a while. Here's how to configure when the Apple TV sleeps:

1. **Select Settings to display the Settings screen.**

2. **Select General to display the General screen.**

3. **Highlight Sleep After.**

4. **Press the Select button one or more times until the interval you want appears.** Your choices are 15 minutes, 30 minutes, 1 hour, 5 hours, 10 hours, or Never.

Configuring General Settings

On the General screen in Settings, you can also set the time zone, choose the language for the user interface, and select accessibility settings. To reach these settings, select Settings ⇨ General from the Home screen.

Setting the time zone

To make sure your Apple TV knows what time it is, make sure the General screen shows the correct time zone. You can either let your Apple TV detect the time zone automatically or set it manually.

Here's how to set the time zone:

1. **On the General screen, select Time Zone.** The first Time Zone screen appears.

2. **If Set Automatically is turned on, highlight it, and then press the Select button to turn it off, as shown in Figure 2.15.**

3. **Select Time Zone.** The second Time Zone screen appears.

4. **Type the first part of the nearest city's name.** Your Apple TV displays a list of matches.

5. **Highlight the appropriate match, as shown in Figure 2.16, and then press the Select button.** The first Time Zone screen appears again with the Time Zone readout now showing the city that you chose.

6. **Press the Menu button to display the General screen again.**

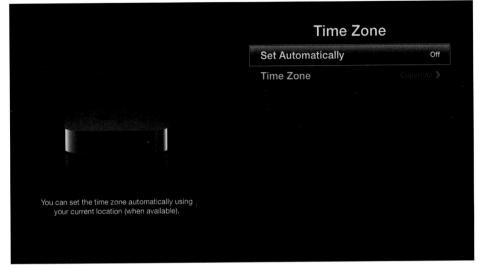

You can set the time zone automatically using your current location (when available).

2.15 On the first Time Zone screen, make sure Set Automatically is turned off.

Time Zone

Closest City:

San F

San Francisco, U.S.A.
Pacific Daylight Time

abc   ABC   #+=   Recent

A   B   C   D   E   F
G   H   I   J   K   L
M   N   O   P   Q   R
S   T   U   V   W   X
Y   Z   1   2   3   4
5   6   7   8   9   0

SPACE   DELETE   CLEAR

2.16 On the second Time Zone screen, type the name of the nearest city, and then select the time zone on the list that appears.

Setting the language

If your Apple TV is already displaying the language you want to use, you're all set. If not, you can change the language by selecting Language on the General screen, and then selecting the language on the Language screen, as shown in Figure 2.17.

Choosing Accessibility settings

If you have trouble reading items on the screen, you can use the Apple TV's VoiceOver feature to read them for you. Here's how to set up VoiceOver:

Language

English
Français
Deutsch
日本語
Nederlands
Italiano
Español
Português (Portugal)
Dansk
Suomi

2.17 Choose the language for the Apple TV's user interface on the Language screen.

1. **On the General screen, select Accessibility.** The Accessibility screen appears.

2. **Select VoiceOver to change the setting from Off to On.** VoiceOver starts announcing the commands you give, starting with "VoiceOver on."

3. **Highlight Speech Rate, as shown in Figure 2.18, and then press the Select button.** Press the Select button one or more times to move through the different speeds: Slow, Medium, Fast, or Very Fast.

4. **Press the Menu button to return to the General screen.**

Accessibility

VoiceOver   On

Speech Rate   Fast

2.18 On the Accessibility screen, you can turn on and adjust the speed of the VoiceOver feature.

Configuring Your iTunes Store account

To make the most of music and video on your Apple TV, you need to link it to your iTunes Store account. This enables you to access content on the iTunes Store, and play the music and videos in your iTunes libraries on your computers after you have set up Home Sharing.

Follow these steps to set up your iTunes Store account:

1. **From the Home screen, select Settings to display the Settings screen.**

2. **Select iTunes Store to display the iTunes Store screen.**

3. **If the Location readout shows the wrong location, select Location, as shown in Figure 2.19, to display the Location screen.** Select your location from the list of countries and regions. Press the Menu button to display the iTunes Store screen again.

iTunes Store

Location	United States
Video Resolution	720p HD
HD Previews	On
Sign In	
Sort Favorites	By Date

2.19 On the iTunes Store screen, you can sign in with your Apple ID to configure your location and other settings.

4. **Highlight Video Resolution, and then press the Select button one or more times to choose the resolution setting that you want.** Your choices are Standard, 720p HD, and 1080p HD.

Genius

For the best picture, choose the highest setting that your Apple TV supports — 1080p HD for the Apple TV model 3 or 720p for the Apple TV model 2. If you find that your Internet connection isn't fast enough to deliver the video stream steadily, choose a lower setting.

5. **Highlight HD Previews, and then press the Select button to toggle between On and Off, as needed.** Normally (unless your Internet connection cannot transfer data fast enough for smooth viewing), you want to view high-definition previews when they are available.

6. **If Sign In appears on the iTunes Store screen, sign in to your account in the following way:**

   ○ **Select Sign In to display the iTunes Store Account screen, as shown in Figure 2.20.**

   ○ **Type your Apple ID, and then select Submit.**

   ○ **On the iTunes Store Password screen, type your password, and then select Submit.**

   ○ **On the Remember Password screen, select Yes if you want your Apple TV to remember your password, or No if you don't.** Your Apple TV signs you in to the iTunes Store. The iTunes Store screen reappears, now showing the Sign Out command and your account name.

iTunes Store Account

abc	ABC	#+=	Recent

To sign in to the iTunes Store, enter your Apple ID. If you don't have an Apple ID, create one using iTunes on your computer by choosing Store > Create Account.

a   b   c   d   e   f

g   h   i   j   k   l

m   n   o   p   q   r   Apple ID:

s   t   u   v   w   x

y   z   1   2   3   4

5   6   7   8   9   0   **Submit**

.   _   @   .com   .net   .edu

SPACE   DELETE   CLEAR

Press ▶ II to change keyboards

2.20 On the iTunes Store Account screen, type your Apple ID, and then select Submit.

Caution Storing your password on your Apple TV is handy if you're the only person who uses it. However, if you share your Apple TV with other people, you may prefer to enter your password manually each time to ensure that you're the only person who can use it.

7. **Highlight Sort Favorites, and then press the Select button one or more times to choose the setting that you want: By Date, Alphabetically, or Off.**

8. **Press the Menu button to return to the Settings screen.**

Choosing a screen saver

Your Apple TV includes a selection of entertaining screen savers that you can set to start after a period of inactivity. You can also personalize the screen saver by using photos from a Flickr account or an iCloud Photo Stream. The Flickr account or Photo Stream can be either your own or someone else's.

Genius

If your TV has a plasma screen, follow Apple's recommendation to use either the Floating screen saver or the Origami screen saver. Floating and Origami cover more of the screen than the other screen savers, so they provide better protection against images getting burnt into the screen. If you don't like either of these screen savers, configure the Apple TV to go to sleep after a short period of inactivity.

Follow these steps to choose and configure a screen saver:

1. **From the Home screen, select Settings to display the Settings screen.**

2. **Select Screen Saver to display the Screen Saver screen.**

3. **Highlight Start After, as shown in Figure 2.21, and then press the Select button to set the interval to wait before starting the screen saver.** Your choices are 2 minutes, 5 minutes, 10 minutes, 15 minutes, 30 minutes, or Never.

Screen Saver

Start After	30 minutes
Show During Music	Yes
Photos	National Geographic
Preview	

Screen Savers

Random

Flip-up

Floating

Holiday Mobile

Origami

Photo Mobile

Floating and Origami are recommended for plasma televisions.

2.21 Choose and configure a screen saver on the Screen Saver screen.

4. **Highlight Show During Music, and then press the Select button to toggle between Yes and No.** Depending on the music that you enjoy, you may find a screen saver a suitable accompaniment.

5. **Select Photos to display the first Choose Photos screen.**

6. **Select the photos to use for the screen saver in one of the following ways:**

   - **To use one of the built-in photo sequences, select National Geographic, Animals, or Flowers, as shown in Figure 2.22.**

   - **To use a Flickr account, select Flickr, and then use the second Choose Photos screen to specify the account.** You can select Add Flickr Contact, as shown in Figure 2.23, type the contact's name on the Add Flickr Contact screen (see Figure 2.24), and then select Submit. You can also select Search, type the contact's name on the Flickr Search screen, and then select Submit.

   - **To use a Photo Stream, select Photo Stream.** If the Photo Stream Setup screen appears, select Yes if you want to turn on Photo Stream for the account that's currently set up on your Apple TV. To use another account, choose No, Use a Different Account, type the name on the Account Name screen, and then select Submit.

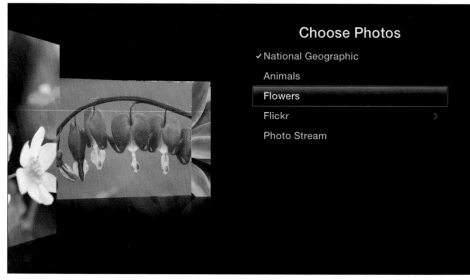

2.22 On the first Choose Photos screen, you can select one of the built-in photo sequences as the source of photos for the screen saver.

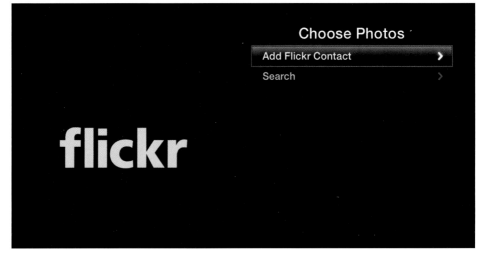

2.23 On the second Choose Photos screen, you can either add a Flickr contact by name or search for a contact.

2.24 On the Add Flickr Contact screen, type the contact's name, and then select Submit.

7. **After Apple TV displays the Screen Saver screen again, scroll down to the Screen Savers section, and then select the screen saver that you want, such as Floating, Origami, or Reflections.**

8. **Whether you select the Ken Burns or Classic screen saver, you have the same controls.** Choose from the following options on the screen that appears:

● **Highlight Time Per Slide, and then press the Select button one or more times to set the number of seconds to play each slide.** Your choices are 2 seconds, 3 seconds, 5 seconds, 10 seconds, and 20 seconds.

Note The Ken Burns screen saver uses zooming and panning over a picture to make it more visually entertaining. Ken Burns is a movie director famous for using this effect in his documentaries.

● **In the Transitions list, select the transition that you want to use, as shown in Figure 2.25.**

● **Press the Menu button to return to the Screen Saver screen.**

Classic

Time Per Slide

Transitions

Random

Cube

Dissolve

Droplet

✓ Fade Through Black

Fade Through White

Flip

Move In

Page Flip

2.25 On the Classic screen, choose the time per slide and transition effect for the Classic screen saver.

Genius Dissolve is the most discreet of the transitions, so it's a good choice if you want to enjoy the pictures without emphasizing the changeover. Many of the other transitions are more dramatic, especially Cube.

9. **Select Preview to preview the screen saver full screen.** Press any button to end the preview.

10. **When you are satisfied with your choices, press the Menu button to display the Settings screen again.**

Choosing Audio and Video Settings

To control how your Apple TV plays back audio and video, you can choose audio and video settings. For example, you can turn the Sound Check feature on or off, apply sound effects, and adjust the HDMI output type and the TV resolution.

Here's how to choose audio and video settings:

1. **From the Home screen, select Settings to display the Settings screen.**

2. **Select Audio & Video to display the Audio & Video screen.**

3. **Highlight Repeat Music, as shown in Figure 2.26, and then press the Select button to toggle between On and Off, as needed.** Selecting On causes the Apple TV to repeat the item you selected to play, such as a playlist or an album.

Audio & Video

Repeat Music	Off
Sound Check	Off
Sound Effects	On
Show Playlists	Music Only
Dolby Digital	Auto
Audio Output	Auto
Audio Language	Default
Subtitle Language	Off
Closed Captioning	Off
HDMI Output	Auto >

2.26 On the Audio & Video screen, you can choose various settings, including Repeat Music.

51

4. **Highlight Sound Check, and then press the Select button to toggle between On and Off, as needed.** Sound Check applies something called *normalization*, which standardizes the volume of the songs as they play.

Genius

Turn on Sound Check to avoid dramatic changes in volume caused when some songs are recorded at a louder volume than others. Turn off Sound Check if you want to experience the full dynamic range of your music, even if that means you have to adjust the volume manually.

5. **Highlight Sound Effects, and then press the Select button to toggle between On and Off, as needed.** Sound Effects include the clicks and bleeps the Apple TV plays when you press the buttons on the Apple Remote; many people find them helpful.

6. **Highlight Show Playlists, and then press the Select button to toggle between Music Only and All.** Choose Music Only if you want to see only the music playlists that your computers are sharing via Home Sharing in iTunes. Choose All if you want to see all of your playlists, including those with videos.

7. **Highlight Dolby Digital, and then press the Select button one or more times to choose the setting that you want: Auto, On, or Off.**

8. **Highlight Audio Output, and then press the Select button to toggle between Auto and 16 bit, as needed.**

Note

For the Audio Output setting, try Auto first. If your TV doesn't receive any sound, switch to 16-bit.

9. **If you need to change the audio language for movies and shows, select Audio Language.** On the Audio Language screen that appears, select the language, as shown in Figure 2.27, or select Default (at the top of the list) to use the default language for each movie or show. When you press the Select button, the Apple TV displays the Audio & Video screen again.

10. **To display subtitles on screen when they are available, select Subtitle Language.** On the Subtitle Language screen that appears, select the language. The Apple TV then displays the Audio & Video screen again.

11. **To use closed captioning, highlight Closed Captioning, and then press the Select button to toggle the setting to On.**

2.27 On the Audio Language screen, select the language that you want to use for audio.

12. **To control the video format the Apple TV uses for output, select HDMI Output.** On the HDMI Output screen that appears, select one of the following output formats, and then press the Menu button to return to the Audio & Video screen:

   - **Auto.** Select this option, as shown in Figure 2.28, to let the Apple TV determine the best format for the TV or monitor to which you connect it. The Apple TV tries YCbCr first. If that doesn't work, it then falls back to RGB High and then RGB Low.

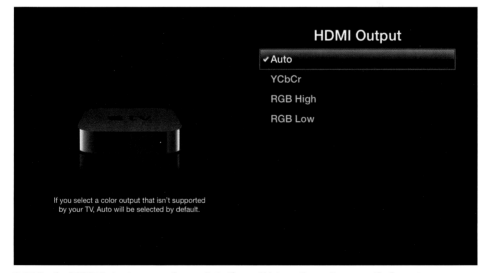

2.28 On the HDMI Output screen, choose Auto if your TV doesn't require a specific format.

53

- **YCbCr.** Select this option to use encoding for video content, such as Blu-ray and DVDs. YCbCr is a mathematical description of a color space. Y stands for the luma or luminance component, which represents the brightness in an image. Cb stands for the blue-difference chroma component, which is the color difference from blue. Cr stands for the red-difference chroma component, which is the color difference from red.

- **RGB High.** Select this option to use settings designed for the red-green-blue (RGB) encoding for standard TVs.

- **RGB Low.** Choose this option to use settings designed for the red-green-blue encoding for PCs.

13. **If you need to change the TV resolution, select TV Resolution.** On the TV Resolution screen, select the resolution that you want. On the Now Displaying screen that appears, select OK if the display is as you want it; otherwise, select Cancel or wait for the Apple TV to automatically switch back to the previous resolution after 15 seconds.

14. **When you finish choosing audio and video settings, press the Menu button to return to the Settings screen.**

Choosing the Proper HDMI Output

If you've connected your Apple TV to a TV via HDMI, select the Auto setting on the HDMI Output screen. This normally provides the best results. If your TV doesn't support YCbCr input over HDMI, the Apple TV switches to RGB High. If you've connected your Apple TV to a computer monitor and the picture looks disappointing, try the RGB Low setting. Because RGB Low uses the color representation designed for computers, the picture should look better.

Avoid using the RGB Low setting with a TV connected via HDMI because it may crush the blacks and blow out the whites, causing the screen to lose detail in the darker and lighter areas.

Setting Up AirPlay

The Apple TV AirPlay feature enables you to play audio and video from your iOS device (that is, an iPhone, iPad, or iPod touch), PC, or Mac on the speakers and TV connected to your Apple TV. If you want only certain people to be able to use AirPlay, you can require them to enter a password.

Follow these steps to set up AirPlay:

1. **From the Home screen, select Settings to display the Settings screen.**

2. **Select AirPlay to display the AirPlay screen shown in Figure 2.29.**

AirPlay

| AirPlay | On |
| Set Password | > |

AirPlay lets you wirelessly view content on your TV from your iPhone, iPad, iPod touch, or iTunes on your computer.

Go to www.apple.com/support/appletv for more information.

2.29 With Airplay turned on, you can play audio and video from an iOS device, or your computer.

3. **If you want to limit AirPlay to people who know a password, select Set Password, type a password on the AirPlay screen that appears, and then select Submit.**

Turning On Home Sharing

The Home Sharing feature enables your Apple TV to access the iTunes libraries you're sharing on your computers. Here's how to set up Home Sharing:

1. **From the Home screen, select Settings to display the Settings screen.**

2. **Select Computers to display the Computers screen.**

3. **Select Turn On Home Sharing, as shown in Figure 2.30.** The Home Sharing Setup screen appears.

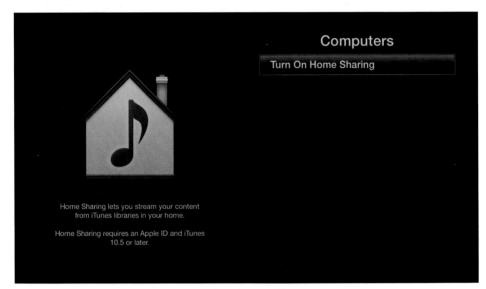

2.30 Turn On Home Sharing to access your shared iTunes libraries.

4. **Select Yes, as shown in Figure 2.31, if you want to use the Apple ID that's already set up on your Apple TV.** To use another account, choose No, Use a Different Apple ID, type the name on the Account Name screen, and then select Submit.

5. **When the Home Sharing Is On screen appears, select OK.** The Computers screen then appears again.

You can now access your shared media by choosing Computers on the Home screen.

Home Sharing Setup

Would you like to use jane_apfelfresser@me.com to turn on Home Sharing on this Apple TV?

Yes

No, use a different Apple ID

2.31 On the Home Sharing Setup screen, choose whether to use the displayed Apple ID or a different one.

See Chapter 4 for more details about Home Sharing.

Note

After you connect your Apple TV to your TV or stereo, you can play music through the TV or stereo speakers. You can use the Apple TV to stream music from your computer, iOS device, or an iTunes library you've put online with iTunes Match. You can also stream the contents of your iOS device's screen via the Apple TV to your TV to play games, or perform other functions. You can build a full music library in iTunes by importing your CDs and adding existing digital audio files.

Playing Music on Your Apple TV 60

Creating a Music Library on Your Mac or PC 60

Playing Music from iCloud 77

Streaming Music to Your Apple TV 86

Streaming the Screen of an iOS Device to Your Apple TV 88

Playing Music on Your Apple TV

Your Apple TV is great for playing music as well as videos. You can play music in the following three ways:

- **Via iCloud and iTunes Match.** iCloud is Apple's online service for storing data and song files. iCloud includes services such as e-mail, calendars and reminders, documents and data storage, and iTunes Match. iTunes Match is a subscription service that enables you to store your entire music library online for easy access. When you set up iTunes Match on your PC or Mac, iTunes scans your music library and identifies which music files are available through the iTunes Store. You can then stream high-quality versions of these files. When songs are in your library but not in the iTunes Store, iTunes uploads copies of them from your library and stores them online for you.

- **Via Home Sharing.** Home Sharing is Apple's technology for sharing your music and other media among your computers and iOS devices. To use Home Sharing, you set up each computer or iOS device with the same Apple ID. After you turn on Home Sharing in iTunes, each computer can access the libraries the other computers are sharing and copy files from those libraries. You can also play music from those libraries on your iPhone, iPad, or iPod touch by streaming the music.

- **By streaming.** You can stream music to your Apple TV from any PC or Mac running iTunes, or from an iPhone, iPad, or iPod touch.

Creating a Music Library on Your Mac or PC

Normally, the best way to get started with music is to create your music library on your main Mac or PC. You can then load the music on your iOS devices and take it anywhere with you; make the music available to your Apple TV via Home Sharing; or simply play the music through the Apple TV using AirPlay from either your computer or your iOS device.

In this section, I first show you how to choose settings for importing your CDs to get great audio quality at a reasonable file size, and how to set iTunes to store your library in a suitable location. Next, I cover importing CDs and adding existing music files to iTunes, converting music files from other audio formats, and creating fixed playlists and Smart playlists that you can enjoy on your computer, iOS device, or Apple TV.

Note

This section shows iTunes running on a Mac, but the dialogs and controls are almost identical in Windows.

Setting iTunes to create high-quality audio files from a CD

Follow these steps to get the best audio quality when you import songs from CD:

1. **Perform the appropriate step below to either open the Preferences dialog (on a Mac) or the iTunes dialog box (on a PC):**

   - **Mac.** Choose iTunes ⇨ Preferences to open the Preferences dialog.

   - **PC.** Choose Edit ⇨ Preferences to open the iTunes dialog box.

2. **Click General in the toolbar to open the General Preferences pane, as shown in Figure 3.1.**

3. **In the When you insert a CD pop-up menu, select one of the following actions:**

3.1 The iTunes General Preferences pane is where you set the action iTunes takes when you insert a CD.

- **Show CD.** This is usually the best choice because it lets you fix any incorrect tag information before you import the CD.

- **Begin Playing.** This setting is good for entertainment but not for importing.

- **Ask to Import CD.** This setting prompts you to import the CD, but normally it's best to check the tag information first and make any changes needed.

- **Import CD.** This setting automatically imports the CD without prompting you.

- **Import CD and Eject.** This setting imports the CD without prompting, and then ejects it without warning. If you use this setting, make sure that your computer's optical drive remains unobstructed.

4. **Select the Automatically retrieve CD track names from Internet check box if you want iTunes to download track names for you.** This is the easiest way to get CD information, but it's a good idea to check that the information is correct before you apply it.

5. **Click the Import Settings button to display the Import Settings dialog.**

6. **In the Import Using pop-up menu, choose the encoder for creating the audio files, as shown in Figure 3.2.** See the next section for advice on choosing an encoder.

Import Settings

Import Using: AAC Encoder

Setting: iTunes Plus

Details

128 kbps (mono)/256 kbps (stereo), 44.100 kHz, VBR, optimized for MMX/SSE2.

☑ Use error correction when reading Audio CDs
Use this option if you experience problems with the audio quality from Audio CDs. This may reduce the speed of importing.

Note: These settings do not apply to songs downloaded from the iTunes Store.

Cancel   OK

3.2 In the Import Settings dialog, you control the quality of the music that you get in iTunes, or on iOS devices and Apple TV.

7. **Choose a quality setting for the encoder in the Setting pop-up menu.** iTunes offers preset choices for all encoders, except Apple Lossless Encoding. To choose custom settings, click Custom and work in the dialog that iTunes displays. Figure 3.3 shows the MP3 Encoder dialog. Here, you can choose custom settings for encoding MP3 files.

MP3 Encoder

Stereo Bit Rate: 320 kbps

☑ Use Variable Bit Rate Encoding (VBR)

Quality: Highest

(With VBR enabled, bit rate settings are used for a guaranteed minimum bit rate.)

Sample Rate: Auto

Channels: Auto

Stereo Mode: Normal

☑ Smart Encoding Adjustments
☑ Filter Frequencies Below 10 Hz

Use Default Settings   Cancel   OK

3.3 The MP3 Encoder dialog lets you choose exactly which settings you want.

8. **Select the Use error correction when reading Audio CDs check box (see Figure 3.2) if you find that your song files contain pops, skips, or dropouts caused by the drive reading them incorrectly, or if you simply want to be sure you get quality audio files.**

9. **Click OK to close the Import Settings dialog, and then click OK to close the Preferences dialog (on a Mac) or the iTunes dialog box (on a PC).**

Genius

Using error correction slows down the importing speed, so some people deselect the Use error correction when reading Audio CDs check box and test whether the song files come out clean. If you're not in a tearing hurry, I suggest that you select this check box to ensure that you don't get unwanted skips and clicks in your songs.

Picking the best encoding for your needs

CDs contain music files in an uncompressed format designed for use on CDs. To copy the songs from CDs to your computer, you use an *encoder* to convert the files to a format suitable for computers. iTunes comes with five encoders, so you can pick the one that's right for your needs. For some of these encoders, you can also adjust the quality setting, or *bitrate*, which also affects the file size.

iTunes comes set to import songs from CD using the Advanced Audio Coding (AAC) encoder at the 256 Kbps bitrate. This provides pretty high audio quality, but you may want to use the Custom dialog to set the highest available bitrate (320 Kbps). If you need to balance audio quality with file size, AAC is usually the best format to choose. iTunes, iOS devices, and the Apple TV all play AAC, but most other hardware and software players can't.

If you want to play your song files on other players, use the MP3 format. It has lower quality than AAC at the same bitrate, so choose at least the Higher Quality (192 Kbps) bitrate for MP3. For best results, use the Custom dialog to set the highest available bitrate, 320 Kbps. If you want the best audio quality and don't care about file size, use the Apple Lossless Encoding encoder. *Lossless* means that, unlike the AAC and MP3 encoders, Apple Lossless Encoding doesn't discard any of the data contained in the original music — so the song files should be perfect. Apple Lossless Encoding files take up much more space than AAC and MP3 files, so you can't fit as much music on your iOS device.

Your last two encoder choices are WAV and AIFF. These are essentially the same as Apple Lossless Encoding in that they are uncompressed, but they have different instructions at the beginning of the file. WAV and AIFF both provide perfect audio quality but lack the tag information that enables iTunes, iOS devices, and the Apple TV to sort them easily. Thus, Apple Lossless Encoding is normally a better choice.

Choosing where to store your library

iTunes is set by default to do the following with your library:

- Put all of your music and video files in the same folder within your Home folder.

- Keep the folder organized by artist folder, album folder, track number, and track title. For example, iTunes would name the first track on Bruce Springsteen's album, *Greatest Hits*, like this: /Bruce Springsteen/Greatest Hits/01 Born to Run.m4a on a Mac or \Bruce Springsteen\Greatest Hits\01 Born to Run.m4a on a PC. (If there's a disc number, such as Disc 1 of 2, iTunes includes that, too.)

- Make a copy of each file that you add to the library from another folder instead of linking to it in that folder.

This behavior is convenient for many people, but if you have a large iTunes library or your computer has a small hard drive, you may run short of space. You may also want to store your iTunes library in a different folder so that you (or others) can access the media files from other computers on your network.

Here's how to check and change where iTunes stores your library, and other key settings:

1. **Perform the appropriate step below to either open the Preferences dialog on a Mac or the iTunes dialog box on a PC:**
   - **Mac.** Choose iTunes ⇨ Preferences to display the Preferences dialog.
   - **PC.** Choose Edit ⇨ Preferences to display the iTunes dialog box.

2. **Click the Advanced button to display the Advanced Preferences pane, as shown in Figure 3.4.** Look at the iTunes Media folder location box to see the folder in which iTunes is storing your music.

3. **If you want to change the folder in which iTunes is storing your music, click the Change button.** The Change iTunes Media Folder Location dialog opens. Select the new folder, and then click Open.

4. **Select the Keep iTunes Media folder organized check box if you want iTunes to organize the folder and file names.** This setting is usually helpful, but it does mean that when you change a tag, such as a song name, iTunes also changes the file name to match.

Advanced Preferences

General Playback Sharing Store Parental Devices Advanced

iTunes Media folder location

/Users/mike/Music/iTunes/iTunes Media

Change...

Reset

☑ Keep iTunes Media folder organized

Places files into album and artist folders, and names the files based on the disc number, track number, and the song title.

☑ Copy files to iTunes Media folder when adding to library

Reset all dialog warnings: Reset warnings

Reset iTunes Store cache: Reset cache

☐ Keep Mini Player on top of all other windows
☐ Keep movie window on top of all other windows

?   Cancel   OK

3.4 Use the Advanced Preferences pane to choose where to store your library.

Genius

If you want to share your media files with other users of your computer, move the iTunes Media folder to a shared folder. For example, on a Mac, you can use a folder in the /Users/Shared/ folder. On a PC, you can use a folder in the \Users\Public\ folder, such as the Public Music window. The disadvantage to sharing your media files is that other users can also delete them.

5. **Select the Copy files to iTunes Media folder when adding to library check box if you want iTunes to copy each file that you add from another folder.** If you want iTunes to create a link to the file in that folder instead, deselect this check box.

6. **Click OK to close the Preferences dialog (on a Mac) or iTunes dialog box (on a PC).**

Importing a CD

After you choose suitable encoding settings and make sure that iTunes stores your library where you want it, you're ready to import your CDs into iTunes. Follow these steps to do so:

1. **Insert an audio CD in your computer's optical drive.** iTunes downloads the CD's information and displays the track listing, as shown in Figure 3.5.

3.5 iTunes displays the CD's track listing so that you can verify the information is correct.

> **Note**
>
> This section assumes that you've chosen the Show setting in the When you insert a CD pop-up menu in the General Preferences pane. If you've chosen one of the Import settings, iTunes either prompts you to import the CD or imports it without asking.

2. **If you need to change the artist, album, or genre, or add the composer, disc number, or year, follow these steps:**

   • **Control+click (or right-click on a PC) the CD in the Devices category in the Source list, and then click Get Info.** The CD Info dialog opens, as shown in Figure 3.6.

3.6 In the CD Info dialog, you can change any of the information.

- **Change the information as needed.** You can change the artist, composer, album, disc number, genre, or year.

Genius

I recommend selecting the Compilation CD check box only if the CD is a compilation by different artists, not if it is a compilation by a single artist. Selecting this check box makes iTunes store the files in the Compilations folder, rather than in the folder with the artist's name. This can make the CD harder to find when you're browsing by artist.

- **Select the Gapless Album check box if the CD has no gaps between tracks.** For example, if it is a live or concept album, you would select this check box to make the tracks play without interruption.

- **Click OK.** The CD Info dialog closes, and iTunes applies your changes to the track listing.

3. **If you need to change the track names, follow these steps:**

- **Control+click (or right-click on a PC) the first track that needs a change, and then click Get Info.** The Information dialog for the song appears, showing the song's name in the title bar, as shown in Figure 3.7.

<!-- Figure: Information dialog -->

Heart of Soul

| Summary | Info | Video | Sorting | Options | Lyrics | Artwork |

Name

Heart of Soul

Artist

Cult

Year

1991

Album Artist

Track Number

7 of 11

Album

Ceremony

Disc Number

1 of 1

Grouping

BPM

Composer

Ian Astbury/William Duffy

Comments

Genre

Rock

☐ Part of a compilation

Previous   Next   Cancel   OK

3.7 The Information dialog for a song includes its name in the title bar.

Genius To change the name of a single track, click the name in the track list to select it, pause a moment, and then click again to open an edit box around it. (Don't double-click — doing so plays the song.) Type the change, and then press Enter or Return to apply it.

- **Type the correct information for the song.** For example, correct the name, change the capitalization, or add a comment to the Comments box.
- **Click Next to display the information for the next song.**
- **When you've made all necessary changes, click OK to close the Information dialog.**

4. **Click Import CD.** iTunes starts importing the CD, and shows its progress at the top of the window, as shown in Figure 3.8.

3.8 iTunes shows its progress as it imports songs from a CD.

5. **When iTunes finishes importing the CD, click the Eject button to the right of the CD's name in the Source list to eject the CD.** The Eject button is the horizontal line with a triangle above it.

You can now remove the CD and insert the next one that you want to import.

Adding existing music files to iTunes

If you already have digital music files, you can add them to your iTunes library easily either by using drag and drop or by using the Add to Library command. Follow these steps to drag and drop music files into iTunes:

1. **Open a Finder window (on a Mac) or an Explorer window (on a PC) and navigate to the folder that contains the files that you want to add to iTunes.**

2. **Arrange the Finder (or Explorer) and iTunes windows so that you can see the Source list in the iTunes window.**

3. **Select the files in the Finder or Explorer window.**

4. **Drag the files to the Library category at the top of the Source list in the iTunes window.** When the mouse pointer displays a plus sign (+), as shown in Figure 3.9, drop the files. iTunes then copies the files to your library and displays the Adding Files dialog shown in Figure 3.10.

3.9 You can add existing music files to iTunes by dragging them to the Library category at the top of the Source list.

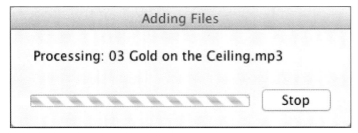

3.10 iTunes displays the Adding Files dialog as it adds music files to your library.

Note If the mouse pointer doesn't display a plus sign (+) when you drag files to the Library category, the files are of a type that iTunes can't play. See the next section for instructions on converting audio files from other formats to those that iTunes can play.

If your computer has a small monitor, or if you prefer working within a single application, you can add your existing music files to your iTunes library by using the Add to Library command. Follow these steps to do so:

1. **In iTunes, choose File ⇨ Add to Library on a Mac, or File ⇨ Add Folder to Library on a PC.** The Add To Library dialog opens, as shown in Figure 3.11.

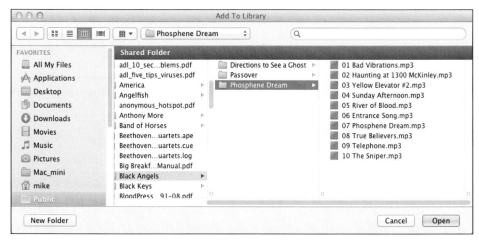

3.11 Use the Add To Library dialog to add existing music files directly to iTunes.

Genius

Instead of choosing File ⇨ Add To Library, you can press ⌘+O on a Mac to open the Add To Library dialog. On a PC, you can choose File ⇨ Add To Library (or press Ctrl+O) when you want to add individual music files (rather than a folder full of music files) to your library.

2. **Navigate to the folder that contains the files that you want to add.**

3. **Choose the item (or items) that you want to add in one of the following ways:**

   - **Add a folder of songs.** Click the folder to select it.

   - **Add individual songs.** To select files, click the first one, and then ⌘+click the rest. If the files are adjacent in the list, click the first one, and then Shift+Click the last.

4. **Click Open on a Mac or Select Folder on a PC.** iTunes closes the Add To Library dialog and displays the Adding Files dialog while it adds the files to your library.

70

Converting music file formats

iTunes can import music files in the following formats:

- **AAC (Advanced Audio Coding).** This is Apple's preferred audio format. It compresses audio and, arguably, offers the best balance of quality and file size.

- **MP3 (MPEG-1 Audio Layer III or MPEG-2 Audio Layer III).** MP3, which is perhaps the most widely used audio format, also compresses audio, and offers a good balance of quality and file size.

- **Apple Lossless Encoding.** This is Apple's full-quality audio format. It uses lossless compression, resulting in smaller audio files than uncompressed audio, but delivers the same quality as uncompressed audio.

- **WAV (Waveform Audio File Format).** Usually referred to simply as WAV, this is a standard PC format for uncompressed audio. Because the audio is uncompressed, it is full quality.

Note WAV files and AIFF files take up more space than compressed formats (such as Apple Lossless Encoding, AAC, and MP3) and don't have tags for storing information (such as the artist and song names), so they're not great for using in iTunes.

- **AIFF (Audio Interchange File Format).** A standard Apple format for uncompressed audio. As with WAV, this uncompressed audio is full quality.

Note iTunes for Windows can import files in the Windows Media Audio (WMA) format, and automatically convert them to the format you set in the Import Settings dialog box. WMA is Microsoft's preferred audio format, and Windows Media Player comes set to copy files to WMA by default. iTunes for OS X cannot import WMA files, so if you have WMA files, you must convert them using either iTunes for Windows or one of the third-party applications discussed in this chapter.

You can add files to iTunes in any of the formats discussed previously. However, to add content in any of the following audio file formats to iTunes, you have to convert them:

- **WMA (Windows Media Audio).** This is the format used by Microsoft's Windows Media Player (usually installed with Windows) and music stores, such as Napster (before 2009). WMA files can be protected with digital rights management (DRM).

- **Ogg Vorbis.** This is a free encoder for compressed audio, roughly comparable to MP3 in quality and file size.

- **FLAC (Free Lossless Audio Codec).** This is a free encoder with full audio quality, roughly comparable to Apple Lossless Encoding in quality and file size.

WMA is widely used, whereas Ogg Vorbis and FLAC are not. The two best approaches for adding unprotected WMA files to iTunes are as follows:

- **If you have access to a PC with iTunes, drag the WMA files from an Explorer window to the library in the iTunes window.** iTunes automatically converts the WMA files to the audio format set in the Importing preferences. Copy the resulting files to your Mac, and then import them into your iTunes library.

- **If you don't have access to a PC with iTunes, use a tool to convert the files to AAC or MP3 on a Mac.** EasyWMA (www.easywma.com) costs $12.99, but also has a demo version available. After converting the files, import them into your library.

Genius

To add protected WMA files to iTunes, you must burn them to CD from Windows Media Player on Windows, and then copy the CD using iTunes. Doing this works, but it contravenes the user agreements of most stores that sell protected WMA files.

The best tool for adding either Ogg Vorbis or FLAC files to iTunes is X Lossless Decoder, or XLD (http://tmkk.pv.land.to/xld/index_e.html), which is not only capable and easy to use but also free. Alternatively, you can use EasyWMA to perform the conversion or the freeware xACT (http://download.cnet.com) to decode the FLAC files to AIFF or WAV, import them into iTunes, and convert them to your preferred format.

Creating fixed playlists and Smart playlists

Sometimes you want to create playlists that contain only the songs you choose, in exactly the order you prefer them. For example, you might burn such a playlist to a CD so you can enjoy it in the car, or publish it to the iTunes Store so that others can enjoy your taste in music. (You can find a discussion of publishing playlists later in this chapter.) At times like this, you need to create a fixed playlist, one that doesn't change unless you change it.

Here's the easiest way to create a fixed playlist:

1. **Select the songs that you want in one of the following ways:**

   - **Click a song to select it.**

   - **Shift+Click to select all of the songs from the one currently selected to the last one that you want.**

   - **⌘+click to add individual songs to the selection.**

2. **Click in the selection, and then drag the songs to the open space at the bottom of the Source list.** iTunes creates a new playlist and puts an edit box around the name.

3. **Type a name for the playlist.**

4. **Click and drag the songs into your preferred order.**

You can also create a fixed playlist by choosing File ➪ New Playlist, naming the playlist, and then clicking and dragging songs to it.

Genius

You can also create a playlist by selecting the songs that you want to include, and then choosing File ➪ New Playlist from Selection from the menu bar.

After creating a playlist like this, you can change it any time you want by adding or removing songs or changing the order of songs. However, unless you make changes, the playlist remains the same — iTunes doesn't change it for you.

Other times, it's more fun to have iTunes create playlists for you. These are called *Smart playlists,* and they can update themselves with new songs. To set one up, you simply tell iTunes what kind of songs you want and how many, and it chooses them for you.

Genius

You can edit any Smart playlist by Control+clicking (on a Mac) or right-clicking (on a PC) it, and then choosing Edit Smart Playlist. This also gives you a peek at the criteria for iTunes' built-in Smart playlists so you can see how they work.

Here's how to create a Smart Playlist:

1. **Choose File ⇨ New Smart Playlist to open the Smart Playlist dialog.** The Smart Playlist dialog starts with just one line of controls, but you can set up a dozen or more conditions if needed.

Genius

On a Mac, you can open the Smart Playlist dialog by Option+clicking the Create Playlist button (+) in the lower-left corner of the iTunes window or pressing ⌘+Option+N.

2. **Set up the first condition using the following controls on the top line:**

   - The first pop-up menu contains about 40 fields of tag data and other information iTunes stores about each song, from Album and Artist, to Composer and Year.

   - The second pop-up menu contains options suitable for the field you set, such as contains, does not contain, is, is not, starts with, and ends with.

   - The text field lets you type text to specify the comparison or details. For example, to create a Smart Playlist of various kinds of rock music, choose Genre in the first pop-up menu, contains in the second pop-up menu, and then type Rock in the text box.

3. **Add other conditions as needed.** Click the Add button (+) to add another line of controls, and then set up your second condition. For example, to get songs from before 2005, choose Year Is Less Than 2005. As soon as you set up two conditions, iTunes replaces the Match the following rule option in the Smart Playlist dialog with the Match all/any of the following rules option.

4. **Choose one of the following options from the Match pop-up menu:**

   - **If you choose all, it makes each condition depend on the one before it.** For example, if the first condition restricts the playlist to songs in the Rock genre, then, from those songs, the second condition can be set to choose only those from 2004 or earlier. From those songs, the third condition can be set to include only songs rated in the four- to five-star range.

- **If you choose any, it applies each condition separately.** For example, the first condition in Figure 3.12 chooses songs that have Bruce Springsteen as the only artist. The second condition chooses songs in which the artist's name includes Tom Petty. So, the playlist will contain songs by Bruce Springsteen, Tom Petty, and Tom Petty and The Heartbreakers (assuming that the library contains songs by all three).

3.12 Choose any in the Match pop-up menu in the Smart Playlist dialog to treat the conditions separately.

5. **Choose whether to restrict your playlist to a certain length or number of songs.** If you want to create a limited playlist, select the Limit to check box. Choose the type of limit in the pop-up menu. Your choices are items, minutes, hours, MB, or GB. Type the number in the text box before it, such as 2 for 2 hours. Choose the selection method in the selected by pop-up menu on the right. Your choices include random, least recently played, or most recently added.

6. **Select the Match only checked items check box if you want to exclude songs with deselected check boxes.** If you deselect its check box when you don't like the song that's playing, you probably want to select this check box.

7. **Select the Live updating check box if you want iTunes to keep updating the Smart playlist.** Automatic updating is one of the most compelling features of Smart Playlists, so selecting this check box is usually a good idea. Other times, though, you may want to create a Smart playlist and not update it.

8. **Click OK to create the Smart playlist.** iTunes adds it to the Source list and displays an edit box around its name.

9. **Type a name for the Smart playlist, and then press Return.**

Genius

Use the Limit to option in the Smart Playlist dialog to create playlists suitable for devices. For example, I use Limit to 700MB when creating Smart Playlists for my 1GB iPod shuffle, which contains about 200MB of data as well. Try using Limit to 70 minutes for creating a playlist to burn to audio CD, or Limit to 20 items for a workout playlist.

The moment you see which songs iTunes has selected for the Smart Playlist, you may realize that your Smart criteria need improving. If so, Control+click (on a Mac) or right-click (on a PC) the Smart playlist's name in the Source list. Choose Edit Smart Playlist to open the Smart Playlist dialog again so that you can tweak the criteria.

To create a more complex Smart Playlist, you can create nested rules that apply only within a particular rule. After you've set up your main rules, click the ellipsis button (…) to the right of the rule under which you want to create nested rules. Here's how this works:

● At the top, the overarching command is Match all of the following rules, as shown in Figure 3.13.

Smart Playlist

☑ Match	all ⬍	of the following rules:		
Last Played ⬍	in the last ⬍	12	months ⬍	⊖ ⊕
Any ⬍	of the following are true			⊖ ⊕
Plays ⬍	is in the range ⬍	0	to 4	⊖ ⊕
Skips ⬍	is greater than ⬍	1		⊖ ⊕
Genre ⬍	contains ⬍	Alternative		⊖ ⊕

☐ Limit to 2 GB ⬍ selected by random ⬍

☐ Match only checked items

☑ Live updating

(?) 　　　　　　　　　　　　　　　　　　　　Cancel　　OK

3.13 You can create nested rules to specify more complex criteria for your Smart playlists.

- The first top-level rule specifies Last Played in the last 12 months. In other words, the song has been played within the last year.

- Under this top-level rule is the any of the following are true condition. This uses two nested rules — the song must match either Plays is in the range 0 to 4 or Skips is greater than 1.

- The second top-level rule specifies Genre contains Alternative, so that any matching song must be in one of the Alternative categories, such as plain Alternative, or Alternative & Punk.

Note You can nest rules up to five levels deep, but you may find that if you set up more than a few, it becomes confusing. Still, it's great to have the power to do this in case you need it one day.

Playing Music from iCloud

Before you can play music on iCloud, you have to put your music on it. Any songs that you buy from the iTunes Store are available on iCloud. You can also easily add all of the other music in your iTunes library by using the iTunes Match feature. At this writing, iTunes Match costs $24.99 per year.

Note If you haven't already set up your iTunes Store account on your Apple TV, do so now. See Chapter 2 for more details.

Setting up iTunes Match on your Mac or PC

To get your music into iCloud, set up iTunes Match on your computer. iTunes then identifies which songs are available in the iTunes Store and enables you to use copies of them. For songs in your library that are not available on the iTunes Store, iTunes uploads copies of them from your computer to iCloud.

Here's how to set up iTunes Match:

1. **In iTunes, click iTunes Match in the Store category of the Source list.** The first iTunes Match screen appears, as shown in Figure 3.14.

3.14 iTunes Match helps you get your music on iCloud.

2. **Click Subscribe for $24.99 Per Year.** The Sign in to subscribe to iTunes Match dialog appears.

3. **Type your password, click Subscribe, and then complete the payment process.**

4. **When the next iTunes Match screen appears, allow iTunes to gather information about your iTunes library, match your music with the songs in the iTunes Store, and then upload the unmatched songs and your custom artwork.**

Note If you have many songs that aren't available in the iTunes Store, iTunes Match can take many hours or even several days to upload copies to the iTunes Store. If you need to stop iTunes Match, click the Stop button on the iTunes Match screen. You can then resume iTunes Match by clicking the Start button that replaces the Stop button.

Playing music from iCloud

Once you have set up your iTunes Store account on your Apple TV, you can play your music from iCloud.

First, follow these steps to turn on iTunes Match:

1. **Go to the Home screen by pressing the Menu button one or more times, as needed.**

2. **Select Music.** The iTunes Match screen appears, as shown in Figure 3.15.

3. **Select Turn on iTunes Match.** Your Apple TV is now ready to stream music from iCloud.

3.15 The iTunes Match screen on Apple TV.

When the iTunes Match screen appears, as shown in Figure 3.16, select the method that you want to use to play your music.

3.16 On the iTunes Match screen, choose how you want to play music or videos.

You can choose from the following options:

- **Shuffle Songs.** Select this item to play songs at random.

- **Search.** Select this item to display the Search screen shown in Figure 3.17. Type your search term, and then select the appropriate result. The list shows Artists first, then Albums, and then Songs.

3.17 On the Search screen, type a search term, and then select the appropriate match in the list.

Note If your search returns many results, either scroll down the list or add characters to your search term to refine the results.

● **Music Videos.** Select this item to display the Music Videos screen, and then select the video that you want to watch.

● **Playlists.** Select this item to display the Music Playlists screen shown in Figure 3.18. This screen lists your playlist folders (if any) first, then your Smart playlists, and finally your fixed playlists. If the playlist that you want is in a folder, select that folder to display its contents, and then select the playlist. Otherwise, simply select the playlist.

Music Playlists

📁	**Artist Playlists** 19 Items	>
📁	**Exercise Playlists** 3 Items	>
📁	**General Playlists** 15 Items	>
📁	**Playlists for Resting** 5 Items	>
📁	**Top Playlists** 2 Items	>
⚙	**Classical Music** 886 Items	>
⚙	**Heavy Metal** 25 Items	>

3.18 On the Music Playlists screen, select the playlist or folder that you want to open.

● **Genius Playlist.** If you select this item, your Apple TV displays the Genius information screen telling you how to use the Genius feature. You can do so in the following two ways:

• **From the Now Playing screen for the song on which to base the Genius playlist, hold down Select to display the menu shown in Figure 3.19, and then select Start Genius.**

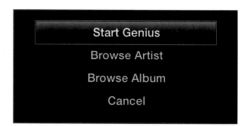

3.19 Select Start Genius to create a Genius playlist from the current song.

• **From any screen that shows a list of songs, highlight the song on which to base the playlist.** Hold down Select to display the menu, and then select Start Genius.

● **Genius Mixes.** Select this item to display the Genius Mixes screen, as shown in Figure 3.20, which contains Genius mixes your Apple TV automatically puts together from your music library. The gray dots at the bottom of the screen indicate the number of mixes available; the white dot indicates which mix is currently selected. Press the Left or Right buttons to highlight the appropriate dot, and then press the Select button to play it.

3.20 Apple TV can create Genius Mixes based on your music library.

⊙ **Artists.** Select this item to display the Artists screen, which provides an alphabetical list of all of the artists in your library, as shown in Figure 3.21. Highlight the artist that you want, and then press the Select button to display that artist's screen, as shown in Figure 3.22. From there, you can either select All Songs to see the full list of songs or select the album that contains the song that you want to play.

3.21 You can browse the artists in your library alphabetically.

3.22 From the screen for a particular artist, you can either display the full list of songs or a specific album.

83

- **Albums.** Select this item to display the Albums screen, which shows an alphabetical list of the albums in your library, as shown in Figure 3.23. Select All Songs to display the full list of songs, or select the album that you want to play.

3.23 From the Albums screen, you can select the album that you want to play.

- **Compilations.** Select this item to display the Compilations screen, and then select the compilation that contains the items that you want to display. You can also select All Songs if you want to browse the full list of songs alphabetically. For example, if you don't remember which compilation contains the song that you're looking for, select All Songs to find it.

Note   The Compilations screen shows the albums that you marked as compilations when importing your CDs, or those that the iTunes Store identifies as compilations. They can either be compilations by the same artist (like a Greatest Hits) or by different artists (such as soundtracks). If you followed my advice not to mark compilations by a single artist as compilations in iTunes, such compilations do not appear in the Compilations list.

- **Songs.** Select this item to display the All Songs screen. Highlight a song to display its details, and then press the Select button to play it.

- **Genres.** Select this item to display the Genres screen. From here, you can select the genre that you want and display the list of artists it contains. Select an artist, and then select the album that contains the item that you want to play.

- **Composers.** Select this item to display the Composers list. You can then browse through the list of composers and select the one whose works you want to display.

Genius Many songs that you import from a CD or download do not have information in the Composer tag. If you want to be able to browse by composer, you will most likely have to use iTunes to add information to the Composer tag for your songs.

Whichever way you browse to the song that you want to play, simply highlight it, and then press the Select button to play it. Your Apple TV displays the song's name and details, along with the album cover (if available) while playing the music, as shown in Figure 3.24.

3.24 The Apple TV displays a song's details and album cover as the music plays.

From here, you can control playback in the following ways with the remote:

- **Press the Select or Play/Pause buttons to pause and resume playback.**
- **Press the Left button to skip back to the beginning of the current song.** Press it again to skip to the start of the previous song.

- **Press the Right button to skip to the beginning of the next song.**

- **Press and hold the Left button to scan backward through a song.** Release the button when you reach the point at which you want to restart playback.

- **Press and hold the Right button to scan forward through a song.** Release the button to restart playback.

- **Press and hold the Select button to display the menu shown earlier in this chapter (see Figure 3.19), and then select one of the following commands:**

  - **Start Genius.** Select this command to create a Genius playlist based on the current song.

  - **Browse Artist.** Select this command to display the artist's complete listing.

  - **Browse Album.** Select this command to display the album's listing.

  - **Cancel.** Select this command to close the menu.

Streaming Music to Your Apple TV

As you saw in the previous section, you can easily play music on your Apple TV by using its Music app and the Apple Remote. But when you're using your computer or your iOS device (your iPhone, iPod touch, or iPad), you can play music from the computer or device through your Apple TV instead.

In this section, I cover how to stream music from your computer — either a Mac or a PC — or from your iPhone, iPod touch, or iPad.

Streaming music from your Mac or PC

To stream music to your Apple TV from your Mac or PC, set the Apple TV as the AirPlay output for iTunes. Follow these steps to do so:

1. **Launch iTunes from the Dock, Launchpad, Start menu, or Start screen as usual.** If iTunes is already running, switch to it by using the Dock or taskbar.

2. **Click the AirPlay button in the lower-right corner of the iTunes window to display the pop-up menu, and then click the Apple TV in the list, as shown in Figure 3.25.**

3.25 Click the Apple TV in the AirPlay pop-up menu in iTunes to stream music from your Mac or PC.

3. **Start playing your music as usual.** For example, double-click the song that you want to hear.

Follow these steps to play music on multiple devices simultaneously:

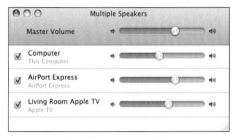

1. **Click the AirPlay button in the lower-right corner of the iTunes window, and then click Multiple Speakers.** The Multiple Speakers dialog appears, as shown in Figure 3.26.

3.26 Use the Multiple Speakers dialog to choose playback devices and set their relative volumes.

2. **Select the check box for each device on which you want to play music.**

3. **Drag the Master Volume control at the top to set the overall volume.**

4. **Drag the volume control for each device you're using to set its relative volume.**

5. **Click the Close button (the red or X button to the left of the title bar) to close the Multiple Speakers dialog.** Alternatively, leave the dialog open so that you can easily adjust the balance of the music.

When you want to switch back to your computer's speakers, click the AirPlay button again, and then click Computer on the pop-up menu.

Note If you like playing music from your computer through your Apple TV, you may want to use other applications, such as Airfoil for Mac or Windows from Rogue Amoeba Software LLC (http://rogueamoeba.com/airfoil/).

Streaming music from your iOS device

To stream music from your iPhone, iPod touch, or iPad to your Apple TV, you simply choose the Apple TV as the AirPlay destination for the Music app. Follow these steps to do so:

1. **Launch or switch to the Music app.** For example, press the Home button to display the Home screen, and then tap Music.

2. **Tap AirPlay to display the AirPlay dialog.** Figure 3.27 shows the AirPlay dialog on the iPad, but it is similar on the iPhone and iPod touch.

3. **Tap the entry for your Apple TV, placing a check mark next to it.** Your iPad, iPhone, or iPod touch can now play music through your Apple TV.

4. **Start the music.** For example, tap Albums, tap the album you want to play, and then tap the appropriate song.

3.27 Tap the entry for your Apple TV in the AirPlay dialog to start playing music.

To switch back from your Apple TV to your iPad, tap AirPlay to display the AirPlay dialog, and then tap iPad. Alternatively, tap AirPlay and then tap a different AirPlay device — for example, another Apple TV, an AirPort Express, or a set of speakers with built-in AirPlay functionality.

Streaming the Screen of an iOS Device to Your Apple TV

Another way to enjoy your Apple TV is to stream the screen of your iOS device to it by using AirPlay Mirroring. This feature can be great for anything from giving presentations to playing games. AirPlay Mirroring works with the iPhone 4S, iPhone 5, iPad 2, the new iPad (also known as iPad 3), the iPad mini, iPod touch fifth-generation, and later models.

Follow these steps to stream the screen from your iOS device:

1. **Connect your iOS device to the same wireless network as your Apple TV.**

Genius

If you have a combination network (that is, one that has both wired and wireless portions), your Apple TV can be connected to the wired portion of the network while the iOS device is connected to the wireless portion.

2. **Press the Home button on the iOS device twice in quick succession to display the recently-used apps bar, as shown in Figure 3.28.**

3.28 Press the Home button twice to display the recently-used apps bar.

3. **Scroll the recently-used apps bar to the left until the music playback controls and AirPlay button appear.**

4. **Tap the AirPlay button to display the AirPlay dialog.**

5. **Tap the Apple TV in the list to place a check mark next to it.** The Mirroring switch appears at the bottom of the dialog.

6. **Tap the Mirroring switch and move it to the On position, as shown in Figure 3.29.** The screen from your iOS device then appears on the TV connected to the Apple TV.

7. **Switch to the iTunes app to display it on the TV.**

When you finish displaying content on the TV, open the recently-used apps bar again, tap the AirPlay button, and then tap iPhone, iPad, or iPod touch, as appropriate.

AirPlay

🖥 iPad

🔊 AirPort Express

🖥 Living Room Apple TV ✓

Mirroring (ON)

With AirPlay Mirroring you can send everything on your iPad's display to an Apple TV, wirelessly.

3.29 In the AirPlay dialog, tap the Apple TV, and then move the Mirroring switch to the On position.

How Do I Set Up and Use Home Sharing?

Home Sharing is On

Your Apple TV will automatically find the iTunes libraries that have Home Sharing turned on using the account " ".

Be sure to use the same account when turning on Home Sharing in iTunes on your computers. Shared computers will appear in Computers on the main menu of Apple TV.

OK

This chapter helps you set up your Apple TV to take advantage of Home Sharing — the powerful music- and video-sharing feature that is built in to iTunes, iOS devices, and your Apple TV. In this chapter, I not only cover what Home Sharing is, but also how to set it up on your Mac, PC, iPhone, iPad, iPod touch, and Apple TV. After you get Home Sharing all set up, you can play content from your shared libraries on your Apple TV. Also, you can control playback from the Apple TV, an iOS device, or iTunes.

Understanding Home Sharing **92**

Setting Up Home Sharing **92**

Playing Content via Home Sharing **98**

Understanding Home Sharing

Home Sharing is an Apple technology for sharing your music and videos among your computers, iOS devices, and Apple TVs. In Home Sharing, the files are stored in the iTunes Media library on one or more computers. By linking an iTunes library to your Apple ID, you turn on Home Sharing and make the library available to other computers and devices linked to the same Apple ID.

Home Sharing lets you share your iTunes library with up to five computers at once. Apple describes these computers as being "authorized" with your Apple ID. So to use Home Sharing, you authorize a computer using your Apple ID.

Note An Apple ID is an online identity that consists of an e-mail address and password. You use the Apple ID to identify yourself to Apple services, such as the iTunes Store, iCloud, and Home Sharing. If you already have an iTunes Store or iCloud account, then you already have an Apple ID; if not, you can set one up in moments by clicking the link in iTunes to create an Apple ID.

Setting Up Home Sharing

The first step is to set up Home Sharing in iTunes on each PC or Mac you will use for sharing. Once you set up Home Sharing on two or more computers, you can copy music and video files among them easily, allowing you to have your full library on each computer. After setting up Home Sharing on your computer, you can also set it up on your iOS devices and your Apple TV.

Setting up Home Sharing in iTunes

Follow these steps to set up Home Sharing in iTunes on each of your Macs or PCs:

1. **Launch iTunes in one of the following ways:**

   - **Mac.** Click the iTunes icon on the Dock. If the iTunes icon doesn't appear on the Dock, click Launchpad on the Dock, and then click iTunes on the Launchpad screen.

   - **Windows.** Choose Start ⇨ All Programs ⇨ iTunes. If the iTunes icon appears on the taskbar, or on the Start menu or Start screen, click the icon there instead.

Note The screens in this section show iTunes on a Mac — however, the user interface for iTunes in Windows is almost identical.

2. **If the Shared category in the Source list is hidden, move the mouse pointer over the word Shared, and then click the word Show when it appears.** The content of the Shared category appears.

3. **In the Shared category, click Home Sharing.** The Home Sharing screen appears.

4. **Type your Apple ID in the Apple ID box and your password in the Password box, as shown in Figure 4.1.**

Genius

If Home Sharing doesn't appear in the Shared category in the Source list, choose Advanced ▷ Turn On Home Sharing from the menu bar.

4.1 On the Home Sharing screen, type your Apple ID and password.

5. **Click Create Home Share.** iTunes contacts Apple's servers for authentication.

6. **If the dialog prompting you to authorize your computer for this Apple ID appears, as shown in Figure 4.2, click Authorize.** Each computer you use for Home Sharing must be authorized. When iTunes completes the authorization request, it displays the Computer authorization was successful dialog shown in Figure 4.3. Click OK.

7. **When the Home Sharing screen reappears with the message that Home Sharing is now on, as shown in Figure 4.4, click Done.**

Home Sharing could not be activated because this computer is not authorized for the account "jane_apfelfresser@me.com". Would you like to authorize now?

Cancel   Authorize

4.2 You may need to authorize your computer before you can use Home Sharing.

Computer authorization was successful.

You have authorized one computer out of your available 5.

OK

4.3 This dialog shows you how many of the five available authorizations you have used.

4.4 When this screen appears, click Done to start using Home Sharing.

You can authorize up to five computers for use with Home Sharing. When you reach the limit of five authorized computers, you must deauthorize one of those before you can authorize another. See the sidebar on how to deauthorize a computer from Home Sharing for further instructions.

Deauthorizing a Computer from Home Sharing

Only five computers can be authorized for Home Sharing, so make sure that you deauthorize any that you no longer have or use. Follow these steps to do so:

1. **Launch or activate iTunes.**
2. **Choose Store ➪ Deauthorize This Computer.** The Deauthorize This Computer dialog appears.
3. **Type your Apple ID if iTunes hasn't stored it.**
4. **Type your password.**
5. **Click Deauthorize.** iTunes deauthorizes the computer, and you can authorize another, if needed.

If you've already gotten rid of a computer or it is no longer working, you must deauthorize all of your computers, and then reauthorize those that you still have. Follow these steps to deauthorize all of your computers:

1. **Launch or activate iTunes.**
2. **Choose Store ➪ View My Account.** The Enter Password dialog appears.
3. **Type your password.**
4. **Click View Account.** The Account Information screen for your account appears in the iTunes window.
5. **Click Deauthorize All.** The Deauthorize Computers dialog appears, asking you to confirm the deauthorization.
6. **Click Deauthorize All Computers.** The Deauthorization Complete dialog appears.
7. **Click Done.**

You now need to reauthorize any computers that you want to use. Choose Store ➪ Authorize This Computer or Advanced ➪ Turn On Home Sharing on each computer, and then follow the prompts.

Caution

Apple allows you to deauthorize all of your computers only once a year, so don't do so just for practice.

Setting up Home Sharing on an iOS device

If you have an iPad, iPhone, or iPod touch, you can set it up to access your Home Sharing libraries, so that you can play the music, videos, and other files from the libraries on your iOS device. To enable access to your Home Sharing libraries, you enter your Apple ID on the iOS device.

Setting up Home Sharing on your iPad

Follow these steps to set up Home Sharing on your iPad:

1. **Press the Home button.** The Home screen appears.

2. **Tap Settings.** The Settings screen appears.

3. **In the left column, tap Music.** The Music screen appears, as shown in Figure 4.5.

4. **Tap the Apple ID field, and then type your Apple ID.** You can tap and hold . (period) to display the list of common domain suffixes, such as .com, .net, and .edu.

5. **Tap the Password field, and then type your password.**

6. **Tap Done.**

4.5 Tap Music to set up Home Sharing on your iPad.

Setting up Home Sharing on your iPhone or iPod touch

Follow these steps to set up Home Sharing on your iPhone or iPod touch:

1. **Press the Home button.** The Home screen appears.

2. **Tap Settings.** The Settings screen appears.

3. **Scroll down to the fifth box (the one that starts with iTunes & App Stores).**

4. **Tap Music.** The Music screen appears.

5. **Scroll down to the bottom of the screen.** The Home Sharing section appears.

6. **Tap the Apple ID field shown in Figure 4.6, and then type your Apple ID.** You can enter the domain suffix quickly by tapping and holding . (period), and then tapping the domain suffix on the pop-up panel.

7. **Tap the Password field, and then type your password.**

8. **Tap Done.**

9. **Either choose further settings on the Music screen or tap Settings to return to the Settings screen.**

Setting up Home Sharing on your Apple TV

At this point, you should set up Home Sharing on your Apple TV if you haven't already done so. You can set up Home Sharing either by working through the Settings app, as described in Chapter 2, or by following these steps:

4.6 Type your Apple ID and password in the Home Sharing section of the Music screen on your iPhone or iPod touch.

1. **Press the Menu button one or more times until the Home screen appears.**

2. **Select Computers.** The first Home Sharing Setup screen appears, as shown in Figure 4.7.

Genius

If you've already set up an Apple ID on your Apple TV, selecting Computers from the Home screen displays a Home Sharing Setup screen that lets you choose between using the existing Apple ID and another Apple ID. Select Yes or No, use a different Apple ID, as needed.

3. **Type your Apple ID.**

4. **Select Submit.** The second Home Sharing screen appears, prompting you to enter your password.

5. **Type your password.**

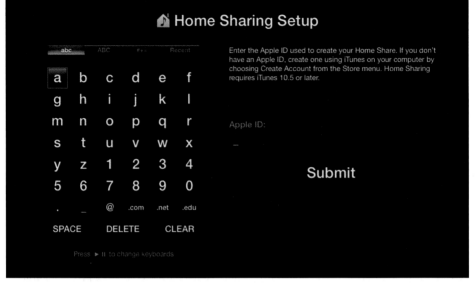

🏠 Home Sharing Setup

| abc | ABC | #+= | Recent |

a	b	c	d	e	f
g	h	i	j	k	l
m	n	o	p	q	r
s	t	u	v	w	x
y	z	1	2	3	4
5	6	7	8	9	0
.	_	@	.com	.net	.edu

SPACE   DELETE   CLEAR

Press ► II to change keyboards

Enter the Apple ID used to create your Home Share. If you don't have an Apple ID, create one using iTunes on your computer by choosing Create Account from the Store menu. Home Sharing requires iTunes 10.5 or later.

Apple ID:

—

Submit

4.7 Select Computers from the Home screen to open the Home Sharing Setup screen.

6. **Select Submit.** The Home Sharing is On screen appears.

7. **Select OK.** Your Apple TV then displays the list of shared libraries on your network. If your network has a single shared library, the Apple TV displays the contents of that library.

Playing Content via Home Sharing

When you've set up Home Sharing on your computers, iOS devices, and Apple TVs, you can play your music and videos — and other items, such as TV shows and podcasts — on any of those devices. You can also copy files easily from one computer's library to another. To play content on a computer, use iTunes; to play music on an iOS device, use the Music app; to play videos, use the Videos app; and to play music and videos on an Apple TV, use the Computers app.

Playing content via Home Sharing on another computer

Follow these steps to play music and videos via Home Sharing on another computer:

1. **Launch or activate iTunes as usual.**

2. **If the Shared category in the Source list is collapsed, move your mouse pointer over it, and then click the word Show that appears.** The content of the Shared category then appears.

3. **Click the shared library to display its contents, as shown in Figure 4.8.** You can then browse the library and play music, videos, and other items as usual. Choose View⇨ Column Browser⇨Show Column Browser to display the Column browser. Then, you can browse the library's contents by genres, artists, and albums.

4.8 After displaying the contents of a shared library, you can browse it and play music or other items.

Copying files from one computer library to another

When you have enabled Home Sharing on two or more of your computers, you can copy files among them easily. This allows you to get all of your music, movie, TV show, book, and app files on each of your computers.

Genius If your computers have enough free space for your entire iTunes library, make sure that you copy all of the files to each computer. Duplicating your library makes it much easier to recover your files if one of your computers suffers a severe failure, such as if the hard drive stops working.

Here's how to copy files from one iTunes library to another:

1. **Use iTunes to connect to the shared library, as described earlier in this chapter.**

2. **In the Show pop-up menu, choose one of the following options:**

   ● **Items not in my library.** Choose this item to restrict the display to items that aren't in the library of the computer you're using.

Genius It's almost always a good idea to choose the Items not in my library option in the Show pop-up menu before copying content from one iTunes library to another. When you copy content, iTunes doesn't check whether the destination library already has it, so if you use the All items option, you can easily end up with duplicate items.

   ● **All items.** Choose this item to display all of the items in the library, whether they're in your computer's library or not.

3. **Select the items you want to import in the following ways:**

   ● **To select a single item, click it.**

   ● **To select a range of contiguous items, click the first, and then Shift+Click the last.**

   ● **To select noncontiguous items, click the first, and then ⌘+click (on a Mac) or Control+click (on a PC) each of the other items.** You can also use this technique to add items to an existing selection or remove items from it.

4. **Click Import.** iTunes imports the selected items to the library on the computer you're using.

Genius If you find your library contains duplicate items after importing from another library, use the File ⇨ Display Duplicates command to make iTunes display a list of files that appear to be duplicates. Double-check that they are in fact duplicates, and then delete them from your library.

You can also set iTunes to automatically import items that you buy from the iTunes Store to your shared libraries. Follow these steps to do so:

1. **Use iTunes to connect to the shared library.**

2. **Click Settings at the bottom of the iTunes window.** The Home Sharing Settings dialog appears.

Note Setting up iTunes to transfer items automatically works only for items you buy from now on. If you've already bought items, you need to copy them manually as described earlier in this chapter.

3. Select the check box next to the type of purchases (Music, Movies, and so on) that you want automatically transferred to your library, as shown in Figure 4.9.

4. Click OK.

4.9 In the Home Sharing Settings dialog, select the check box for each type of purchase that you want automatically transferred to the computer library.

Playing content via Home Sharing on Apple TV

Follow these steps to play music or videos via Home Sharing on your Apple TV:

1. **From the Home screen, select Computers.** The Computers screen appears, and lists your library (or libraries) in one of the following ways:

   - If your network has multiple libraries, Apple TV shows the Computers list shown in Figure 4.10.
   - If your network has only one shared library, Apple TV shows that library's contents and you can proceed to Step 3.

2. **Select the library that you want to open.** That library's contents appear, as shown in Figure 4.11.

3. **Browse and play the content in the following ways**:

   - **Select Music.** The list of music appears.
   - **Select Albums.** The Albums list appears.
   - **Select the album that you want to play.** The album's contents appear.
   - **Select the song that you want to play.**

4.10 If you have multiple libraries, the Computers screen lists them for you.

4.11 When you select a shared library, its content appears.

Playing content via Home Sharing on an iOS device

You can also play your shared music on your iPhone, iPod touch, or iPad. This can be a great way to use your iOS device to enjoy music that won't fit on it because of its space constraints. Even better, you can use AirPlay on your iPhone, iPod touch, or iPad to play music stored on your computer through speakers connected to your Apple TV, AirPort Express, or other AirPlay-enabled device.

Playing content via Home Sharing on an iPhone or iPod touch

Follow these steps to play music via Home Sharing on your iPhone or iPod touch:

1. **Press the Home button.** The Home screen appears.

2. **Tap Music.** The Music screen appears.

3. **Tap More.** The More screen appears, as shown in Figure 4.12.

4. **Tap Shared.** The Shared screen appears.

5. **Tap the shared library that you want to use, as shown in Figure 4.13.** That library's content then appears, as shown in Figure 4.14.

6. **Browse the library and play music.** Browse the Artists listing, tap to display the album list, tap to display an album, and then tap a song to play it.

To play videos, use the same technique with the Videos app.

4.12 On your iPhone or iPod touch, tap the More button on the toolbar to display the More screen.

4.13 On the Shared screen, tap the library that you want to view.

4.14 The contents of the shared library then appear.

Playing content via Home Sharing on an iPad

Follow these steps to play music via Home Sharing on your iPad:

1. **Press the Home button.** The Home screen appears.

2. **Tap Music.** The Music screen appears.

3. **Tap More.** The More panel appears, as shown in Figure 4.15.

4. **Tap Shared.** The Shared panel appears, as shown in Figure 4.16.

5. **Tap the shared library that you want to open.** That library's contents appear, as shown in Figure 4.17.

To play videos, use the same technique with the Videos app.

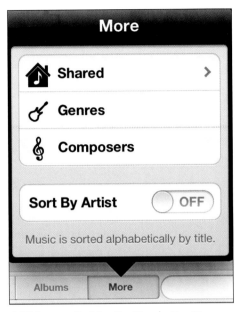

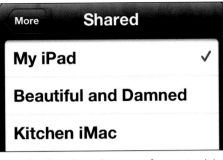

4.16 The Shared panel appears after you tap it in the More panel.

4.15 On your iPad, tap the More button to display the More panel.

4.17 After opening the shared library, you can browse its contents and play music.

Once it is connected to your large-screen TV or monitor, your Apple TV is ready for its main purpose — playing high-quality video content over your network or Internet connection. In this chapter, I show you how to make the most of movies and videos on your Apple TV. You can watch movies, TV shows, and trailers from Apple's iTunes Store. You can also view content from Netflix, Hulu Plus, and the Vimeo video-sharing website. I begin by reviewing how you can find the types of video content that you want.

Choosing How to Watch Movies and Videos 108

Using the Movies App... 109

Using the TV Shows App 114

Using the Trailers App 119

Watching Movies and TV Shows on Netflix 121

Watching Videos on Hulu Plus..................................... 123

Watching Videos on Vimeo... 127

Choosing How to Watch Movies and Videos

On your Apple TV, you can access movies and videos in the following ways:

● **Movies app.** This app gives you access to the movies available in the iTunes Store. You can preview movies, and rent or buy them. You need an Apple ID to use this app.

Note A lot of video content has geographical restrictions applied to it. For example, many movies have different release dates in different countries and regions. For this reason, the content available in most of the Apple TV video apps varies depending on your location.

● **TV Shows app.** This app gives you access to the TV shows available in the iTunes Store. You can preview shows and buy them. You need an Apple ID to use this app.

● **Trailers app.** This app gives you access to the movie trailers available on the iTunes Store. You don't need an Apple ID to watch trailers.

● **Netflix app.** This app gives you access to the content available on the Netflix video-streaming service for your geographical region. You must subscribe to Netflix to use this app.

● **Hulu Plus.** This app gives you access to the content available on the Hulu video-streaming service for your geographical region. You need to subscribe to the Hulu Plus subscription service to use this app.

● **Vimeo.** This app gives you access to the content available on the Vimeo video-sharing site. You can browse the videos on Vimeo without creating an account, but you need one to get the most out of the service. A basic account is free and gives you all of the features you need to use Vimeo on the Apple TV.

Watching movies and videos online can be frustrating, because not all movies, TV shows, or other video content are available from all sources. This is usually because of licensing restrictions imposed by the content creators and distributors (such as movie studios). As a result, you most likely need to use several apps and sources to find the content that you want to watch on your Apple TV.

Caution If you have children, you can restrict access to the movie and video content on your Apple TV. This is most likely a good idea, as renting or buying content can quickly become expensive. The movie and video apps also give viewers access to content that's not suitable for children. For more details about setting up parental controls on your Apple TV, see Chapter 2.

Using the Movies App

Your Apple TV can access a wide variety of movies available on the iTunes Store. Most movies are available for either rental or purchase. You can preview a movie to decide whether you want to rent or purchase it.

Note If the HD symbol appears, the movie is in high definition. If you have a third-generation Apple TV, that is 1080p. If you have a second-generation Apple TV, that is 720p.

The following list explains how to browse and watch movies using the Movies app:

● **Open the Movies app.** To start watching movies, open the Movies app by selecting Movies from the Home screen. The Movies app opens and the Movies screen appears, as shown on the opening page of this chapter.

● **Find movies with the Top Movies list.** To see which top movies are available, select Top Movies at the top of the Movies screen. The Top Movies screen appears, and displays the Top Movies and New & Noteworthy lists. Scroll further down the screen to view other lists, such as Great Documentaries, Great Franchises, Pixar Classics, and others.

Note If no Buy button appears for the movie, then it is most likely still at the stage within the release window when distributors make it available for renting only. Check back in a few weeks.

● **Browse movies by genre.** If you're looking for a particular type of movie, select Genres from the Movies screen to browse by genre. On the Genres screen, shown in Figure 5.1, select the one that you want to view, such as Action & Adventure. On the resulting screen, shown in Figure 5.2, select the movie for which you want to see more details.

5.1 Select the genre that you want to explore.

5.2 Within a genre, you can explore lists, such as the Top, and New & Noteworthy lists.

◉ **View information about a movie.** When you find a movie that you want to learn more about, select it. Its screen then appears, as shown in Figure 5.3, with more details about it. From this screen, you can preview or rent the movie, add it to your wish list, or view more information. If the Buy button appears, you can purchase the movie. Select More to display the More screen, as shown in Figure 5.4. In this screen, you can navigate among reviews and information about the actors, director, producers, and screenwriters. Press the Menu button to return to the movie's screen.

5.3 From a movie's screen, you can preview, rent, or buy it.

5.4 The More screen displays reviews for a movie, and information about the actors, director, producers, and screenwriters.

Previewing and renting movies

Before you rent or buy a movie, chances are you want to preview it. To preview a movie, select Preview from the movie's screen. The preview starts playing full screen. You can pause and resume playback by pressing the Play/Pause button, or skip backward and forward by pressing the Left and Right buttons. When the preview finishes, Apple TV displays the movie's screen again.

To rent a movie, select Rent from the movie's screen. The Rent screen appears, as shown in Figure 5.5, spelling out the terms of the rental. Select OK if you want to go ahead and watch the movie, and it starts playing.

Rent 'Wanted'

You are about to rent 'Wanted' in HD with Dolby Digital 5.1.
You'll have 30 days to start watching the movie. After you start the movie, you'll have 24 hours to finish it.

This movie can only be viewed on Apple TV.

OK

Cancel

5.5 On the Rent screen, read the terms of the rental, and then select OK if you want to proceed.

Caution The standard terms for renting a movie give you 30 days to start it. However, once you start the movie, you have only 24 hours in which to watch it. So, you don't get to dip into a rented movie, and then decide to watch it the following week (unless you're prepared to pay again).

Buying a movie

To buy a movie, select Buy from the movie's screen. The Buy screen appears, as shown in Figure 5.6, and explains that you can either watch the movie on your Apple TV, or download it with iTunes to watch on your computer, iPhone, iPod touch, or iPad.

Note Buying movies on your Apple TV is fast and easy, and being able to download a copy to iTunes to watch on your computer or iOS device is great. However, the movie file is still heavily restricted compared to a DVD containing the same movie. Unlike with a physical DVD, you cannot resell the movie file, or even give it to someone else to play.

Buy 'The Hunger Games'

You are about to buy 'The Hunger Games' in HD with Dolby Digital 5.1.

You can view this purchase on your Apple TV. You can also use iTunes to download it for viewing on your computer or iOS device.

OK

Cancel

5.6 On the Buy screen, select OK if you want to purchase the movie.

Searching for movies or finding them with Genius

When you know which movie you want, usually the easiest way to reach it is by searching. Select Search from the Movies screen to display the Search iTunes Store Movies screen, as shown in Figure 5.7. You can then type your search term and select the result that you want to view.

Search iTunes Store Movies

Search for:

comma_

| abc | ABC | #+= | Recent |

a	b	c	d	e	f
g	h	i	j	k	l
m	n	o	p	q	r
s	t	u	v	w	x
y	z	1	2	3	4
5	6	7	8	9	0

SPACE   DELETE   CLEAR

Press ► ‖ to change keyboards

The Ten Commandments
Released 1956

Commando (1985)   [HD]
Released 1985

Wing Commander: The Movie   [HD]
Released 1999

Command Performance (2009)   [HD]
Released 2009

Command Decision
Released 2007

5.7 On the Search iTunes Store Movies screen, type the search term, and then select the result to view.

Your Apple TV's Genius feature recommends movies based on those you have watched on your iTunes Store account. Genius analyzes the movies you have rented and purchased, and suggests similar or related movies. To see the Genius recommendations, select Genius from the Movies screen. The Genius screen appears, showing the Movies for You heading at the top and a list based on your previous movie selections below.

Genius

Once you've performed a few searches, you can use the Recent keyboard on the Search screen to quickly enter your search terms again. Press the Play/Pause button one or more times until the Recent keyboard appears, or select the Recent tab at the top of the keyboard area.

Creating a Wish List and using the Purchased list

To track movies you'd like to watch, you can add them to your Wish List. To do so, select Wish List on the movie's screen and the Apple TV adds it to your Wish List. The Wish List button then changes to a Remove button that you can select if you decide to remove the movie from your Wish List. To view your Wish List, select Wish List from the main Movies screen.

Note

The Wish List item appears on the Movies screen only when you have added one or more items to your Wish List.

When you buy a movie, Apple TV adds it to the Purchased list in the Movies app. To return to a movie that you've purchased, select Purchased from the Movies screen. The Purchased screen appears, and then you can quickly navigate among your movies.

Using the TV Shows App

Along with movies, the iTunes Store provides a wide selection of TV shows that you can watch on your Apple TV. You can browse shows by using the Top TV Shows list, or you can browse by network or genre, get recommendations from the Genius feature, or simply search for shows by keyword or name.

To watch TV shows, select TV Shows from the Home screen. The TV Shows screen appears, as shown in Figure 5.8. From here, you can browse by using the Top TV Shows, Networks, or Genres lists. Alternatively, you can use the Search feature to find shows or get recommendations from the Genius feature.

5.8 From the TV Shows screen, you can browse by Top TV Shows, Networks, or Genres.

Browsing and Finding TV Shows

You can browse TV shows in the following ways:

- **Use the Top TV Shows list.** To find the latest or most popular programs, select Top TV Shows at the top of the TV Shows screen. You can then browse the Top TV Shows list, the Latest TV Episodes list (which appears further down the screen), or the Kids TV Shows Under $10 list (which appears even further down).

- **Browse by network.** If you know which network hosts the show that you want, or if you prefer some networks to others, you can browse TV shows by network. Select Networks at the top of the TV Shows screen to display the TV Networks & Studios screen, as shown in Figure 5.9, and then select the network or studio that

TV Networks & Studios

Discovery Channel

Disney Channel >

ESPN >

Food Network >

FX >

History Channel >

IFC >

Lifetime >

MTV >

National Geographic >

Nickelodeon

5.9 On the TV Networks & Studios screen, select the network or studio that produces the show that you want to watch.

115

produces the shows that you want to browse. On the screen for a network or studio (see Figure 5.10) you can browse through its shows. To see details about a program, select it.

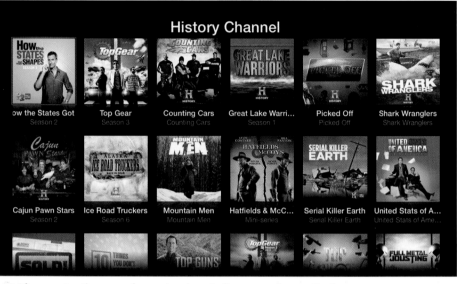

5.10 After opening the screen for a network or studio, you can browse its shows.

⊙ **Browse TV shows by genre.** To find TV shows of a particular type, select Genres at the top of the TV Shows screen. You can then select the appropriate genre on the Genres screen, shown in Figure 5.11. You can choose from Animation, Classic, Comedy, Drama, Kids, Nonfiction, Reality TV, Sci-Fi & Fantasy, or Sports. On the screen that appears, you can browse lists for that genre, including Top TV Shows, Latest TV Episodes, and New & Noteworthy.

⊙ **Find TV shows with Genius.** As with movies, the Apple TV Genius feature analyzes the TV shows that you have previously rented or purchased, and suggests similar or related shows. To see the Genius recommendations, select Genius from the TV Shows screen.

Genres

Animation	>
Classic	>
Comedy	>
Drama	>
Kids	>
Nonfiction	>
Reality TV	>
Sci-Fi & Fantasy	>
Sports	>

5.11 On the Genres screen, select the genre of TV shows that you want to browse.

• **Search for TV shows.** As with movies, the easiest way to find a specific TV show is to search for it by name. Follow these steps to do so:

1. **From the TV Shows screen, select Search.** The Search iTunes Store TV Shows screen appears.

2. **Type your search term or terms.** A list of results appears.

3. **Select the result that you want to view.** The screen for that TV show appears.

Genius

When searching, remember to use the Recent keyboard — you can save time and effort by using it to re-enter search terms you've used before.

Viewing show information and finding episodes

When you find a TV show that you want to learn more about, select it. The screen for that show appears, as shown in Figure 5.12. From this screen, you can play an episode, add the show to your favorites, buy a season pass, or explore other seasons.

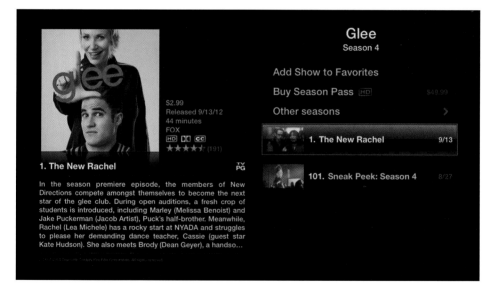

5.12 From the screen for a TV show, you can select the episode that you want to watch.

If the episode that you want to watch appears on the TV show's screen, select it to display its information screen, as shown in Figure 5.13. From here, you can preview or buy the show. If the episode doesn't appear on the TV show's screen, select Other Seasons to display the seasons list, and then select the appropriate one. You can then select the episode to display its information screen.

1. The New Rachel
Glee, Season 4

In the season premiere episode, the members of New Directions compete amongst themselves to become the next star of the glee club. During open auditions, a fresh crop of students is introduced, including Marley (Melissa Benoist) and Jake Puckerman (Jacob Artist), Puck's half-brother. Meanwhile,...

Released 9/13/12
44 minutes
FOX
HD DO CC
★★★★⯪ (191)

$2.99
Preview   Buy HD

Viewers Also Watched

5.13 From the screen for an episode, you can preview or buy it.

Genius

If the episode's description is truncated, press the Up button to display the rest of it, which appears in place of the release date, length, and other details. Press the Up button again to go back to the details.

Watching previews and adding shows to Favorites

After locating the episode that you want to watch, you can also preview it before buying it. To preview an episode, select Preview from the episode's screen. The preview starts playing full screen. You can pause and resume playback by pressing the Play/Pause button, and skip backward and forward by pressing Left and Right.

When the preview finishes, the Apple TV displays the episode's screen again. If you want to buy the episode, select Buy from the episode's screen. The Buy screen appears, explaining that you can either watch the show on your Apple TV or download it with iTunes to watch it on your computer, iPhone, iPod touch, or iPad.

To track TV shows that you want to view, navigate to a show's screen, and then select Add Show to Favorites. The Apple TV adds the show to your Favorites list, and then displays the Remove from Favorites button in place of the Add Show to Favorites button.

Returning to previously purchased TV shows

When you buy a TV show, your Apple TV adds it to the Purchased list in the TV Shows app. To return to a TV show that you've purchased, select Purchased from the TV Shows screen. The Purchased screen appears, and you can quickly navigate among your shows.

Using the Trailers App

To remain informed about upcoming movies and decide which ones you want to watch, you can view trailers. From the Home screen, select Trailers to open the Trailers app, as shown in Figure 5.14. Browse to the trailer that you want to view, and then select it.

5.14 In the Trailers app, select the trailer that you want to view.

On the screen for the movie trailer, as shown in Figure 5.15, select Play to start playback.

5.15 On the trailer's screen, select Play to watch it.

To see more information and video content for the movie, select More. On the screen that appears, you can view further content, such as more trailers and behind-the-scenes footage, as shown in Figure 5.16.

5.16 Many movies have additional content that you can view, such as more trailers and TV spots.

Watching Movies and TV Shows on Netflix

In addition to content from the iTunes Store, your Apple TV can also display content from Netflix. Netflix is a subscription service for streaming video. At this writing, Netflix costs $7.99 per month, but it offers a one-month free trial so you can give the service a spin. Netflix works on Apple TVs, computers, iPhones, iPads, and iPod touches. You can set up a Netflix account using your Apple TV, but if you have a computer handy, you may find the process easier to set up that way. You need a valid credit or debit card, or a PayPal account that's linked to a valid card.

To get started with Netflix, select Netflix from the Home screen. On the opening screen, select the Start Your 1 Month Free Trial button if you want to try the free trial, and then complete the process for signing up. If you already have a Netflix account or if you used your computer to set up a free trial, select the Already a member? Sign in button. Sign in on the Netflix screen that appears, and then select Submit. On the screen that follows, type your Netflix password, and then select Submit again.

Selecting movies and shows

After you sign in to Netflix, you see the Home screen, as shown in Figure 5.17.

5.17 From the Netflix Home screen, you have several browsing options.

From there, you can choose any of the following options to navigate Netflix:

- **Genres.** Selecting this option displays the Genres screen. You can then select the genre you want to browse, such as Foreign Movies.

- **TV Shows.** Select this option to display the TV Shows screen, which separates shows into categories, such as TV Dramas, TV Comedies, and TV Sci-Fi & Fantasy.

- **New Releases.** This option displays the New Releases screen, as shown in Figure 5.18, which presents a scrollable list of new items.

5.18 The New Releases screen presents a straightforward list of new videos.

- **Just for Kids.** Select Just for Kids to display the Just for Kids screen. You can then choose Suggestions to view selected children's shows, Characters to browse by character (such as SpongeBob SquarePants or Thomas the Tank Engine), or Search Kids to search for children's shows by name or keyword.

- **Search.** Select this option to display the Search screen, on which you can type your search terms and browse matching results.

- **Sign Out.** When you're finished using Netflix, select Sign Out from the Netflix home screen, and then select Yes on the confirmation screen that appears.

Viewing information about or watching a video

When you find a movie or show that you're interested in, select it to display its information screen, as shown in Figure 5.19.

5.19 Select the item you're interested in to open its information screen.

From here, you can select any of the following options:

- **Play.** Selecting this option starts the movie or show.

- **Rate.** Select this option, press the Left or Right button to set the number of stars (from one to five), and then press the Select button.

- **More.** When selected, this option displays a screen with more information about the actors in the video and its category. Select an actor or actress to display other movies that feature that person.

Watching Videos on Hulu Plus

Hulu Plus is a subscription service for streaming video across the Internet. Hulu Plus offers a wide choice of movies and TV shows. To get started with Hulu Plus, you need to create an account. You can sign up for a free trial using your Apple TV, but because you need to enter several items of information, it's usually easier to use a computer if you have one. Open your preferred web browser, go to the Hulu website (www.hulu.com), and then click the Sign Up link. Complete the sign-up procedure (you need a credit card or a PayPal account), and then return to your Apple TV when your account is live.

Note Hulu has free accounts for its basic service, which is called Hulu. However, to use Hulu on your Apple TV, you must subscribe to the Hulu Plus service. At this writing, Hulu Plus costs $7.99 per month. Hulu offers a one-week trial subscription to let you test-drive the service.

On the Hulu Plus screen on the Apple TV, select the Already a Hulu Plus subscriber? Log in button. On the resulting screen, type your e-mail address and select Submit. On the next screen, type your password, and then select Submit again.

Choosing movies and shows

After you sign in to Hulu Plus, you see the Hulu Plus Home screen, shown in Figure 5.20.

5.20 The Hulu Plus Home screen appears after you sign in to your account.

From here, you can select from the following options to navigate Hulu Plus:

- **Popular and Recommended.** If you want to be able to keep up with talk at the water cooler, this is a good place to start. Selecting this option displays the Popular and Recommended screen, which contains categories, such as Shows You Watch, Featured, Recommended for You, Popular Shows, and Popular Movies.

- **Recently Watched.** If you leave a show before it ends or want to view an item again, select Recently Watched from the Hulu Plus home screen to display the Recently Watched list. There, you can review the items you've watched and quickly start watching any of them again.

- **TV.** Select this option to display the TV screen, as shown in Figure 5.21. From here, you can browse using the Popular and Recommended, Genres (from Action and Adventure, to Sports and Videogames), Networks, or A–Z (which makes it easy to find shows by name) lists.

5.21 On the TV screen, choose the way in which you want to browse Hulu Plus for TV shows.

● **Movies.** Selecting this option displays the Movies screen, shown in Figure 5.22. From here, you can browse using the Popular and Recommended, Genres, or Criterion Collection (a selection of recently added and popular movies) lists. You can also view the list of available movie trailers or the A–Z list of all available movies.

5.22 On the Movies screen, choose how you want to browse titles.

● **Trailers.** Selecting this option displays the Trailers screen, which gives you easy access to trailers split into lists, such as Most Popular, Recently Added, and Now Playing.

● **Search.** Select this option to display the Search screen, type your search term, and then examine the results.

● **Sign Out.** When you finish using Hulu Plus, select Sign Out from the Home screen to exit the service.

Note The Favorites and Queue item appears on the Hulu Plus home screen after you have selected + Queue for an item. Select Favorites and Queue to display your Favorites and Queue list.

Viewing information about and playing a video

When you find a movie or show you want to learn more about, select it. The information screen for the movie or show then appears. For a TV show, you can then select the episode to display its information screen, as shown in Figure 5.23. From here, you can select Play to play the video, or add it to your Favorites and Queue list by selecting + Queue.

5.23 From an item's information screen, you can play it or queue it for future play.

Watching Videos on Vimeo

Vimeo is a video-sharing website to which members can upload videos. You can watch videos on Vimeo without becoming a member, but to get the most out of it, you should set up an account. Having an account enables you to upload videos (from your computer, not your Apple TV) and create your own channel.

Vimeo is a free service, but you can also create paid accounts. A Vimeo Plus account ($9.95 per month) includes features such as priority uploading. If you want to be able to upload videos in full 1080p quality, you can go for a Vimeo PRO account ($199 per year).

Caution Vimeo includes videos that are not suitable for children. If you allow your children to use Vimeo, supervise their use of the service. To prevent your children from using Vimeo, set up parental controls as discussed in Chapter 2.

At this writing, you can't set up a Vimeo account using the Vimeo app on the Apple TV — you must use your computer. To set up a free account, open your computer's browser, go to http://vimeo.com/join, and then fill in the form. You must accept the terms of service and provide a verifiable e-mail address. Once you've done this, Vimeo sends you an e-mail message. Click the Complete Your Registration button in the message to finish setting up your account.

If you want to link your Vimeo account to your Facebook account, click the Join with Facebook link on the Join Vimeo page.

Launching the Vimeo app and signing in

To launch the Vimeo app on your Apple TV, select it from the Home screen. The Vimeo Home screen then appears, as shown in Figure 5.24. If you have a Vimeo account, sign in by select-ing Sign In, typing your Vimeo name (your e-mail address) on the screen that appears, and then selecting Submit. On the following screen, type your Vimeo password and select Submit again. Vimeo authenticates you and then displays your Vimeo name on the Sign Out button, which replaces the Sign In button on the Home screen. If you don't have a Vimeo account, you can browse and search for videos, but you can't use any of the *my* features because they are linked to individual accounts.

vimeo

Featured Channels	>
Categories	>
Watch Later	>
My Feed	>
My Videos	>
My Likes	>
Search	>
Sign In	

5.24 Select the Vimeo app on your Apple TV to open the Vimeo Home screen.

Browsing for content

To find videos to watch, you can browse using the Vimeo Featured Channels screen or Categories list. To browse by featured channels, select Featured Channels on the Home screen. The Featured Channels screen, shown in Figure 5.25, presents lists, such as Vimeo Staff Picks, Vimeo Video School, Everything Animated, Independent Filmmakers, and Music Videos.

To browse by category, select Categories from the Home screen. You then see the Categories screen, as shown in Figure 5.26, which shows a wide range of categories in alphabetical order. When you find an interesting item, select it to display its information screen. From there, you can play the video or take other actions, as discussed later in this chapter

5.25 The Featured Channels screen contains lists, such as Vimeo Staff Picks.

5.26 In the Vimeo Categories screen, you can browse categories in alphabetical order.

Genius If an item interests you, but you don't want to watch it now, select Later to add it to your Watch Later list. When the time comes to catch up on your viewing, go to the Home screen and select Watch Later to display the My Watch Later screen, from which you can select the items you've marked.

You can also browse Vimeo using the following options from the Home screen:

- **My Feed.** Select this option to display videos Vimeo recommends for you based on what you've watched.
- **My Videos.** This option displays the videos you've uploaded to Vimeo.
- **My Likes.** Select this option to display videos for which you've selected the Like button.

Searching for and playing videos

As with other video services, you can search for videos on Vimeo. Select Search on the home screen to display the Search screen, type your search term, and then browse the results. When you find a video that you want to learn more about, select it, and its information screen appears, as shown in Figure 5.27.

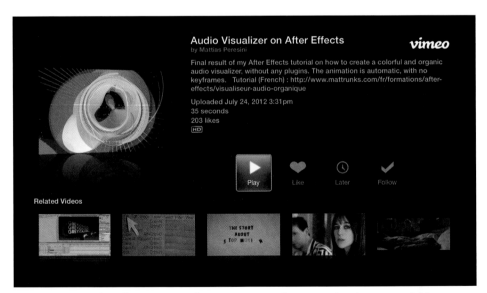

5.27 Selecting a video takes you to its information screen where several options are available.

You can then take any of the following actions:

- **Play.** Select this option to play the video.

- **Like.** To add a video to your My Likes list, select this option.

- **Later.** Selecting this option adds the video to your Watch Later list.

- **Follow.** Select this option to follow the user who made the video. Vimeo then sends you details about new videos the user uploads.

To toggle the display of the details, press the Up button.

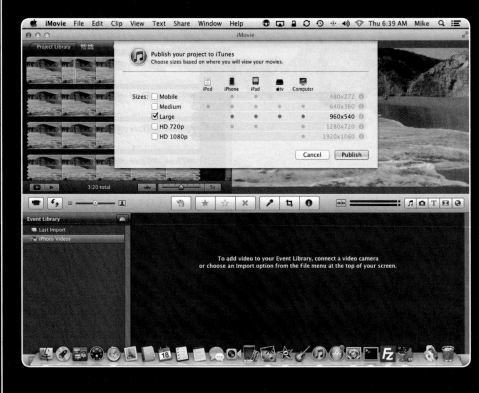

To make the most of your Apple TV, you can play your own movies and videos on it. You can play your own content using the Apple TV to access shared items in your iTunes libraries, or by using AirPlay to send content from a computer or iOS device to the Apple TV. In this chapter, I cover how to create videos on an iOS device, Mac, or PC; how to create video files from video clips; how to convert videos; and how to copy files from DVDs. First, though, I explain which video formats your Apple TV can play.

Understanding Which Video Formats Your Apple TV Can Play **134**

Checking Whether a Video Will Play on Your Apple TV **134**

Creating Videos with Your iOS Device **136**

Creating Files from Video Clips on a Mac or PC **136**

Converting Video File Formats **137**

Creating Video Files from DVDs **140**

Understanding Which Video Formats Your Apple TV Can Play

Your Apple TV can play the following video formats, each at up to 30 frames per second:

- **H.264.** The third-generation Apple TV can play H.264 at up to 1080p. The second-generation Apple TV can play H.264 at up to 720p.
- **MPEG-4.** This format plays up to 720×432 (432p) or 640×480.
- **Motion JPEG.** This format plays up to 720p.

Note The designation 1080p refers to video that uses 1080 lines of horizontal resolution and progressive scan, rather than interlacing. The 720p designation is used for video that uses 720 lines of horizontal resolution and progressive scan. Progressive scan draws each line of the image in sequence, from the top to the bottom of the frame. Interlacing draws the odd and even lines of the image alternately. Progressive scan looks better than interlacing.

The list is short enough to seem straightforward, but in practice the formats tend to be confusing. This is because each format is really a family of different formats that use different file extensions. For example, Apple favors its QuickTime technology for multimedia. However, a QuickTime file isn't a single file type but, rather, it is a multimedia file containing different types of tracks. One track contains the video, another supplies the audio, another adds the effects applied to the tracks, and so on. So a QuickTime file, which typically has the .mov file extension, may contain different types of audio and video tracks.

Note Generally speaking, the Apple TV and iTunes can play QuickTime and MPEG-4 movie files that have the file extensions .mov, .m4v, or .mp4. They can also play protected video content you buy or rent from the iTunes Store.

Checking Whether a Video Will Play on Your Apple TV

Usually, the easiest way to find out if your Apple TV will be able to play a particular video file is to try adding it to iTunes. If iTunes accepts the file and can play it, you'll be able to play the file on your Apple TV, either from iTunes or from the Apple TV.

You can add a video file to iTunes in either of the following ways:

- **Drag the file from a Finder or Explorer window.** This is usually the better method, because you can see whether iTunes accepts the file or not. If iTunes displays a plus sign (+) when you drag the movie file to the Library section of the Source list, as shown in Figure 6.1, iTunes adds the file. If the plus sign (+) doesn't appear, iTunes can't handle the video file and rejects it.

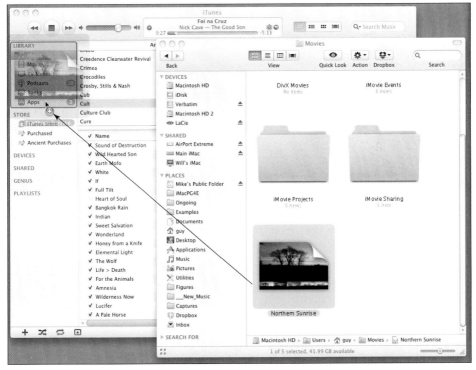

6.1 Drag a video file to the Library section of the iTunes Source list to add it to your library.

- **Use the Add to Library dialog to add a file to your library.** The problem with this method is that iTunes doesn't give you any indication of whether it has accepted the file or not — there's also no error message if it rejects the file. Follow these steps to add a file:

    1. **Choose File ⇨ Add to Library.** The Add to Library dialog opens.

    2. **Navigate to the file, and then click it to select it.**

    3. **Click Open.** iTunes adds the file.

135

Note If you have a Mac, you can use other apps, such as Beamer, to play movie formats on your Apple TV that iTunes can't. See Chapter 11 for information on Beamer.

Creating Videos with Your iOS Device

If you shoot a video on your iPhone, iPad, or iPod touch, you can play it back on your Apple TV without needing to change it. To play the video back on your Apple TV, open the video either in the Camera app or in the Videos app, tap the Share button at the bottom of the screen, and then tap the button for your Apple TV. You can then tap the Play button to start playback.

If your video has extra footage at the beginning or end, you can cut the file down to size with the Trim feature in the Camera app. If the video needs more work than that, you can import it into iMovie on the iOS device and edit it there.

If you have a Mac, you can import the video from your iOS device into iMovie and manipulate it there, and then export it to a suitable format, as discussed later in this chapter. Similarly, if you have a PC, you can import the video into Windows-based video-editing software, edit the movie there, export it, and convert it to a format you can play on your Apple TV.

Creating Files from Video Clips on a Mac or PC

If you shoot video clips on your digital camera, you can create Apple TV–friendly movies in both Windows and OS X. To create video files from video clips on a Mac, use iMovie. After importing your clips and editing them into your video, follow these steps to export the video:

1. **If the movie project isn't open, click it in the Project Library to select it.**
2. **Choose Share ⇨ iTunes.** The Publish your project to iTunes dialog appears.

Note iMovie is part of iLife, the multimedia software suite Apple includes with all new Macs. iMovie is easy to use and has strong features, so it's a great place to start working with video. If you need more powerful editing and production capabilities and effects, consider buying Final Cut, Apple's pro-quality video-editing software.

3. **In the Sizes column, select the check box for each size that you want to create, as shown in Figure 6.2.** Look at the tv column to see which sizes are compatible.

4. **Click Publish.** iMovie creates the video file and adds it to your iTunes library.

6.2 In the iMovie Publish your project to iTunes dialog, select the check box for each movie size that you want to create.

After shooting video clips on your video camera or digital camera, you can import them into Windows Live Movie Maker on a PC, and then edit and arrange them into a video. When the video is finished, follow these steps to export it to a file in the Windows Media Video (WMV) format:

1. **In Windows Live Movie Maker, choose File ⇨ Save Movie.** The Save Movie panel appears.

2. **Click For Computer in the Common Settings area.** The Save Movie dialog appears.

3. **Type a name for the exported video file.**

4. **Select the folder in which to save the video file.**

5. **Click Save.** Windows Live Movie Maker exports the video file to the folder that you chose.

Windows Live Movie Maker exports the video file in the WMV format. Neither iTunes nor your Apple TV can play this format, so you'll need to convert the video file as described later in this chapter.

Converting Video File Formats

If you have video files that iTunes can't play, try using HandBrake. HandBrake is a free file-conversion app that can convert many video formats into files that iTunes and your Apple TV can play.

Genius

HandBrake is a powerful tool, but if it doesn't meet your needs, you can find many other file-conversion utilities online. Many of these are marketed to particular niches (for example, file converters for Apple TV, or file converters for iPhone) and are relatively expensive for the features that they offer. Others harbor spyware, adware, or malware. It's a good idea to research any such tool carefully before downloading and installing even a trial version of it.

To get HandBrake, download the installation file from the HandBrake website (http://handbrake.
fr) and install it on your computer in one of the following ways:

● **Mac.** If OS X doesn't automatically open a Finder window showing the contents of the
HandBrake disk image, click the Downloads icon on the Dock, and then click the
HandBrake disk image file on the Downloads stack that opens. In the Finder window
showing the contents, drag the HandBrake icon to your Applications folder.

● **PC.** Either allow your browser to run the installation file, or double-click the file to run it
after the download completes. Click the Yes button in the User Account Control dialog
box that Windows displays, and then follow the screens of the HandBrake Setup Wizard.

Genius

On a Mac, if you also install the free video player called VLC, you can use HandBrake
to extract files from DVDs.

After installing HandBrake to your Applications folder, run it from the Windows Start menu or from
the OS X Launchpad screen. You can then convert files by following these steps:

1. **Click the Source button on the toolbar.** The Open dialog appears.

2. **Select the file that you want to convert, and then click Open.** The file's details appear
in the HandBrake window.

3. **Open the Title pop-up menu, and then click the title that you want to convert.**

Note

A *title* is one of the recorded items on a DVD. If you're converting a DVD, you can easily identify the main title by its length, which is the same as the movie itself (such as
2 hours). If you're converting a video file, it normally contains only one title.

4. **Optionally, select the part of the file that you want to convert in the following ways:**

   ● **Angle.** If the file contains multiple angles, open this pop-up menu, and then choose
   the angle.

   ● **Chapters, Seconds, or Frames.** Open this pop-up menu, and then choose Chapters,
   Seconds, or Frames, as needed.

   ● **Start through End.** After selecting Chapters, Seconds, or Frames, use these controls to
   specify the starting and ending chapters, seconds, or frames. For chapters, these controls are pop-up menus containing the chapter numbers in the file or DVD. For seconds
   or frames, these controls are text boxes in which you type the appropriate values.

5. **In the Destination area, look at the folder and file name that HandBrake is set to use for the converted file.** If necessary, you can change the folder by clicking the Browse button, selecting the folder, and then clicking Save. You can rename the file by simply typing a different name.

6. **If the Presets pane doesn't appear on either side of the HandBrake window, click Toggle Presets at the right end of the toolbar.** The Presets pane appears, as shown in Figure 6.3.

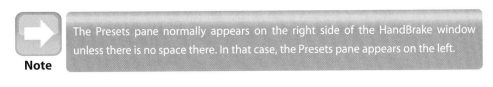

6.3 In the HandBrake Presets pane, choose the preset to use for the file you're converting.

> The Presets pane normally appears on the right side of the HandBrake window unless there is no space there. In that case, the Presets pane appears on the left.
>
> **Note**

7. **If the Devices category in the Presets pane is collapsed, click the disclosure triangle to expand it.**

8. **Click the preset that you want to use.** For example, click AppleTV 3 to create a file suitable for the third-generation Apple TV.

9. **If necessary, choose different settings on the tabs in the lower half of the HandBrake window.** To start with, try the default settings and see what results they produce.

10. **Click Start near the left end of the toolbar to start the conversion.**

Creating Video Files from DVDs

If you have DVDs, you may want to play them on your computer, iOS devices, and Apple TV. This section outlines options for converting DVDs to files that you can easily play. However, you might be wondering why iTunes can't import video from DVDs. After all, iTunes is great at importing music from CDs.

Understanding the legalities of copying DVDs

The problem with importing commercial DVDs is that doing so is normally a violation of copyright law. Unless you get permission from the copyright holder to import a specific DVD, doing so is usually illegal. To avoid exposing themselves to lawsuits for encouraging violations of copyright, major companies don't provide DVD-importing apps.

Caution Don't copy commercial DVDs without getting permission. The penalties for violating copyright law can be harsh.

If you create your own DVDs and retain the copyrights to them, it is fine for you to import them. In fact, you may not need to import them from the DVDs — chances are you have digital files that you can easily convert to an iTunes-friendly format. The following sections cover some of the best tools for importing DVDs on a Mac or PC.

Note Some Blu-ray and SD DVDs include an iTunes digital copy that you can import into iTunes.

OS X tools for copying DVD files

At this writing, the best tool for copying DVDs on a Mac is HandBrake, which I covered earlier in this chapter. To copy a DVD with HandBrake, you must install VLC (www.videolan.org), a free app for playing videos and DVDs. HandBrake uses VLC's capabilities to decrypt DVDs.

HandBrake includes a preset for creating files suitable for Apple TV, so you can easily create the right kind of files. Figure 6.4 shows HandBrake copying a DVD that I created.

6.4 HandBrake is an OS X tool for copying DVDs.

Note

Riplt from The Little App Factory (http://thelittleappfactory.com/ripit/) is another tool for copying DVDs. It creates DVD files on your Mac's hard drive. This is great if you want to be able to play DVDs from your Mac, but you still have to convert those files to use them on the Apple TV. Riplt costs $24.95, but there's a free trial version you can test before buying.

141

Windows tools for copying DVD files

The following tools are available for copying DVD files in Windows:

- **Any Video Converter Ultimate.** At this writing, this converter from DVDSmith, Inc. (http://dvdsmith.com) is available for $59.95. It copies DVD files and also includes a converter that performs a wide variety of video format conversions. It also features presets for Apple devices, including the iPad, iPod, and Apple TV. Download the trial version to see if you like it. Figure 6.5 shows Any Video Converter Ultimate preparing to copy a DVD.

- **AnyDVD and CloneDVD.** AnyDVD from SlySoft (www.slysoft.com) is a decryption utility that enables your computer to read a DVD. To actually copy a DVD, you need another SlySoft program, such as CloneDVD or CloneDVD mobile. Using these two programs, you can copy DVDs to formats that work with iTunes and Apple TV. To get started, download the 21-day trial versions.

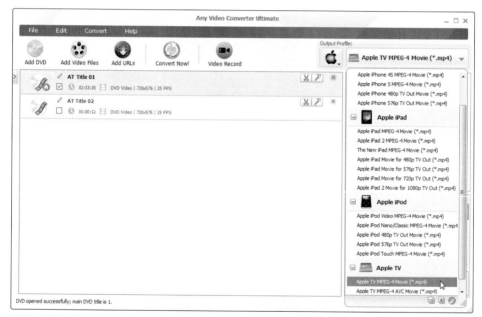

6.5 Any Video Converter Ultimate is a Windows tool for copying DVDs.

How Can I Listen to the Radio and Podcasts on My Apple TV?

Radio

Categories

Adult Contemporary >

Alternative Rock >

Ambient >

Blues >

Classic Rock >

Classical >

College/University >

Comedy >

Country >

Eclectic

As covered earlier in this book, your Apple TV is great for watching movies and videos. But it's also great for listening to Internet radio and catching up on the news, views, and latest music. Your Apple TV comes with a wide range of Internet radio stations, but you can also play unlisted stations using your computer. You can also use your Apple TV to watch or listen to podcasts, episodic programs you can find in huge quantities on the Web. Some podcasts are audio-only, but others use video, so you can make the most of the Apple TV's audio-visual capabilities.

Listening to the Radio 146

Listening to Podcasts 150

Listening to the Radio

If you enjoy listening to the radio, you'll appreciate the wide range of radio stations your Apple TV can deliver. Because the radio stations are transmitted through the Internet rather than the airwaves, you can listen to stations from anywhere in the world with the same ease.

Genius

Audio-only podcasts can be similar to Internet radio programs. The big difference between Internet radio and audio podcasts is that Internet radio is broadcast in real time, so you can listen only to the current shows rather than dipping into an archive and starting the programs at will. By contrast, you can play podcasts on demand, stopping and restarting them as needed.

Opening the Radio app and finding stations

To start listening to Internet radio, select Radio from the Apple TV's home screen. The Radio screen appears (see the opening pages of this chapter), showing a list of radio categories that range alphabetically from Adult Contemporary and Alternative Rock, to 70s Retro, 80s Flashback, and 90s Hits. Select the category that you want to browse and its screen appears, as shown in Figure 7.1.

7.1 On the screen for the radio category, select the station that you want.

Select the radio station that you want to listen to, and its screen then appears, as shown in Figure 7.2. The station starts playing.

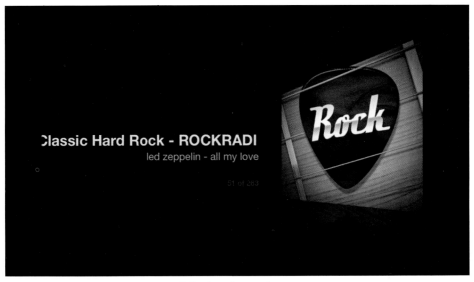

Classic Hard Rock - ROCKRADI
led zeppelin - all my love

51 of 263

7.2 After the station starts playing, settle back and enjoy the music.

After you start playing a radio station, you can quickly browse through other stations in the same category. To jump to the next station in the list and start playing it, press the Right button. To jump to the previous station, press the Left button.

Creating a list of favorite radio stations

When you find a radio station that you like, add it to your Favorite Stations list. To add the station, play it, and then hold the Select button until the dialog shown in Figure 7.3 appears. Select Add Station to Favorites to add the station to the list.

Add Station to Favorites

Cancel

7.3 Hold the Select button until this dialog appears to add a station to your Favorite Stations list.

After you add the first radio station to your favorites, the Favorite Stations list appears near the top of the Radio screen, as shown in Figure 7.4. From here, you can quickly select one of your favorite stations.

Radio

Now Playing

Favorite Stations

MetalHeart

BLUES TRAIN

Instrumental Breezes

Categories

Adult Contemporary   >

Alternative Rock   >

Ambient   >

Blues   >

Classic Rock

7.4 The Favorite Stations list appears near the top of the Radio list.

Playing an unlisted station

Your Apple TV has an impressive list of Internet radio stations, but you may also want to listen to stations that don't appear on the list. You can't do this directly on your Apple TV — but if you have a computer, you can play the station easily using iTunes. You can then send the output to your Apple TV via AirPlay, so you have the station playing on the Apple TV.

Here's how to open another radio station in iTunes:

1. **Find the station's URL.** The easiest way to do this is to go to the station's website and look for the link.

2. **Copy the URL.** For example, select it, Control+click (or right-click on a PC), and then click Copy on the context menu.

3. **Open iTunes or switch to it.**

4. **In iTunes, choose Advanced ⇨ Open Stream.** The Open Stream dialog appears.

5. **Type or paste the URL for the radio station, as shown in Figure 7.5, and then click OK (or press Enter or Return).** iTunes tunes into the radio station and it starts playing (see Figure 7.6). You can control playback of the radio station using the iTunes controls.

7.5 Type or paste the URL for the radio station's stream in the Open Stream dialog in iTunes.

6. **Click the AirPlay button in the lower-right corner of the iTunes window and choose your Apple TV from the pop-up menu.** iTunes starts streaming the radio station to the Apple TV.

7.6. The radio station starts playing in iTunes.

Genius

To give yourself easy access to the radio station, add it to a playlist. The easiest way to add the station to a new playlist is to drag it from where it's playing to open space below the Playlists category in the Source list. You can also click the New Playlist button (the + button) in the lower-left corner of the iTunes window to create a new playlist, give it a name, and then drag the radio station to it.

149

Listening to Podcasts

Internet radio can be great, but you're stuck with the broadcasters' schedules — you can't rewind to the start of a show you've caught in the middle, let alone choose from a menu of programs to start when you want. By contrast, podcasts are available on demand, so you can start playing a podcast at any time that suits you. You can fast-forward the podcast, rewind it, or play the whole thing time after time if you want.

Finding podcasts

To find out which podcasts are available, select Podcasts from the Apple TV home screen. The Podcasts screen appears, as shown in Figure 7.7. Here, you can browse by Top Podcasts, Genres, Providers, or by searching.

7.7 You can browse the available podcasts in several ways from the Podcasts screen.

You can browse podcasts in the following ways:

- **Top Podcasts.** Select this option to open the Top Podcasts screen, as shown in Figure 7.8. This screen contains various lists of podcasts, starting with the New & Noteworthy list. At the top of the screen, select the All tab to view all podcasts, the Audio tab to view only audio podcasts, or the Video tab to view only video podcasts.

7.8 Use the Top Podcasts screen to browse for podcasts.

- **Genres.** Select Genres from the Podcasts screen to display the Categories screen, as shown in Figure 7.9. After you select a genre, you see a screen of podcasts broken into lists, as shown in Figure 7.10. Browse the New & Noteworthy, What's Hot, or All Podcasts lists to find those that interest you.

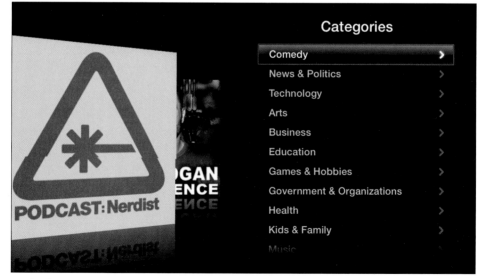

7.9 On the Categories screen, select the genre of podcasts that you want to browse.

Technology

All   Audio   **Video**

New & Noteworthy

MacBreak Weekly — Leo Laporte & Friends
iPad Today — Leo Laporte & Sarah Lane
TECH NEWS TODAY — with Tom Merritt
iFive for the iPhone — with Sarah Lane
iFive for the iPhone — with Sarah Lane

Always On How-To MacBreak Weekl... iPad Today (HD) Tech News Toda... iFive for the iPho... iFive for the iPho...
CNET.com TWiT TWiT TWiT TWiT TWiT

What's Hot

Apple Keynotes
TEDTALKS ►VIDEO — IDEAS WORTH SPREADING
applebyte
RAILSCASTS
TWiT LIVE SPECIALS — Leo Laporte & Friends
TEDTALKS ►HD — IDEAS WORTH SPREADING

Apple Keynotes TEDTalks (video) The Apple Byte (... RailsCasts TWiT Live Speci... TEDTalks (hd)

7.10 On a genre's screen, you can browse the lists of podcasts.

- **Providers.** If you know who created the podcast that you want, select Providers from the Podcasts screen. The Featured Providers screen appears, as shown in Figure 7.11. Select the provider to display that provider's screen. Figure 7.12 shows the screen for The New York Times.

- **Search.** To search for a podcast, select this option from the Podcasts screen. On the Search iTunes Store Podcasts screen that appears, type your search term. As you type, the screen displays matching results. Select a result to display that podcast's details.

- **All, Audio, and Video tabs.** Use the tab bar at the top of the screen to switch among viewing all podcasts, only audio

Featured Providers

MORE Broadcasting
NASA   >
NBC News   >
NEWSWEEK.com   >
The New Yorker   >
The New York Times   **>**
Nickelodeon   >
NPR   >
The Onion   >
PBS   >
PBI

7.11 On the Featured Providers screen, select the one with the podcasts that you want to browse.

podcasts, and only video podcasts. Press the Up button to move the highlight up to this bar, and then press the Left or Right buttons as needed to select the tab that you want. When the tab's contents appear, the Apple TV automatically moves the highlight down from the tab bar so that you can start browsing the podcasts without switching tabs unintentionally.

7.12 Some providers, like The New York Times, offer a wide range of podcasts.

Viewing information about or playing a podcast

When you find a podcast you want to learn more about, select it. Its screen then appears, as shown in Figure 7.13, and displays a list of available episodes, as well as brief details about the one that is highlighted.

7.13 On a podcast's screen, select an episode to view more details about it.

When you select an episode, its screen appears, as shown in Figure 7.14. It contains information about the podcast and a list of related podcasts. If you want the podcast to play, select Play. You can then control playback as normal by using the Play/Pause, Left, and Right buttons on the Apple Remote.

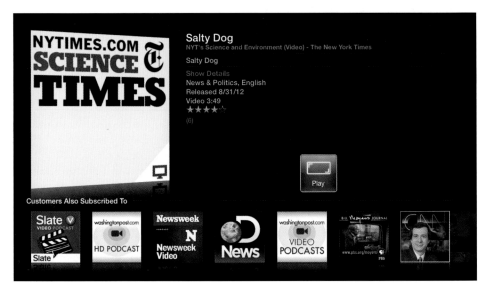

7.14 On an episode's screen, select Play to start playback.

Finding unlisted podcasts

Your Apple TV can access a wide range of podcasts, but nothing like the full range available on the Internet. For example, while browsing the Web, you may discover interesting podcasts you want to watch. You can't add podcasts to the list on your Apple TV (unless Apple happens to add them). However, you can follow these steps to open podcasts in iTunes on your computer, and then send the output via AirPlay to your Apple TV:

1. **Copy the podcast's URL.** For example, Control+click (or right-click on a PC) the URL, and then click Copy on the context menu.

2. **Open iTunes (or switch to it if it's already running).**

3. **Choose Advanced ⇨ Subscribe to Podcast.** The Subscribe to Podcast dialog opens.

4. **Paste the URL, as shown in Figure 7.15, and then click OK (or press Enter or Return).** iTunes adds the podcast to your library.

5. **With Podcasts selected in the Library category of the Source list, move the mouse pointer over the podcast, and then click the Play Selected button that appears, as shown in Figure 7.16.** The podcast starts playing.

6. **Click the AirPlay button in the lower-right corner of the iTunes window and choose your Apple TV from the pop-up menu.** iTunes streams the podcast to the Apple TV.

Subscribe to Podcast

URL:

http://www.nasa.gov/rss/NASAcast_vodcast.rss

Cancel   OK

7.15 Type or paste a podcast's URL in the Subscribe to Podcast dialog, and then click OK.

MOBTOWN SKA SOUNDS
1 Episode

Play Selected ●

NASACast Video
1 Episode

TALK SHOW

The Talk Show
2 Episodes

7.16 Click the Play Selected button to start a podcast.

Making Your Own Podcasts

As mentioned earlier in this chapter, podcasts can consist of only audio or full-motion video produced to professional specifications. They can also fall somewhere in between, such as a video podcast with some still photos, some talking-head video, and other video footage, as needed.

What's in the podcast is the podcast producer's choice — and you can easily be that podcast producer. If you have a Mac, you almost certainly have the applications you need to create a podcast because each new Mac comes with GarageBand and iMovie. (If your Mac doesn't have these applications, you can buy them from the App Store.)

GarageBand is great for recording and mixing audio, and for creating soundtracks to accompany video footage. iMovie gives you powerful tools for importing, preparing, and mixing video, and adding audio tracks. If you have a PC, you can create podcasts with Windows Movie Maker (on Windows XP or Windows Vista) or Windows Live Movie Maker (on Windows 7 or Windows 8).

What Can I Do with Photos on My Apple TV?

Apple's Photo Stream feature is a great way to get more enjoyment out of your photos. Setting up Photo Stream on your computers, iOS devices, and your Apple TV gives you easy access to your photos. In this chapter, I cover how Photo Stream works, and how to set it up so that your computers and iOS devices automatically upload your photos to your iCloud account. You can then view your Photo Stream on the TV or monitor connected to your Apple TV. This chapter also shows you how to browse photos on the Flickr service.

Understanding Photo Stream 158

Setting Up Photo Stream...158

Viewing Photos with Photo Stream 166

Browsing Photos on Flickr.......................................169

Understanding Photo Stream

Photo Stream is an Apple feature for sharing your latest photos online by using your iCloud account. You can share the photos either with only yourself (or, more precisely, your iCloud account) or with others. Photo Stream can share up to 1,000 photos taken within the last 30 days. Once you have turned Photo Stream on, the feature automatically puts your latest photos online in your iCloud account. From there, your computer, your iOS devices, and your Apple TV can access the photos, enabling you to view them anywhere.

The photos in Photo Stream can come from the following sources:

- **Your iPhone, iPad, or iPod touch.** Any photos that you take using the Camera app on an iOS device go into the Camera Roll album, and Photo Stream then picks them up from there.

Note
Pictures that you save from e-mail messages or from web pages on your iOS device also go into your Camera Roll, so that they, too, show up in Photo Stream.

- **A digital camera you connect to your computer.** When you import photos from your digital camera into iPhoto on a Mac or the folder you've designated for Photo Stream on your PC, your computer automatically adds them to your Photo Stream.
- **Images that you manually add to your Photo Stream.** On a Mac, you can drag any image to the Photo Stream item in the Recent category in the iPhoto Source list to add it. In Windows, you can copy or move any photo to the folder that you've designated for Photo Stream.

Setting Up Photo Stream

In this section, I show you how to set up Photo Stream on your computer (Mac or PC), your iOS devices (iPad, iPhone, and iPod touch), and your Apple TV.

Setting up Photo Stream on a Mac

Here's how to set up Photo Stream on your Mac:

1. **Choose Apple ⇨ System Preferences.** The System Preferences window opens.

2. **In the Internet & Wireless section, click iCloud.** The iCloud preferences pane appears. If you're not currently signed into iCloud, the pane displays the sign-in controls, as shown in Figure 8.1. If you are currently signed into iCloud, skip to step 4.

8.1 Type your Apple ID and password in the iCloud preferences pane, and then click Sign In.

3. **Type your Apple ID and password, and then click Sign In.** OS X signs in to your iCloud account, and then displays the full set of controls in the iCloud preferences pane.

4. **Select the Photo Stream check box, as shown in Figure 8.2.**

8.2 In the iCloud preferences pane, select the Photo Stream check box.

159

5. **Click Options.** The Photo Stream Options dialog appears.

6. **Select the My Photo Stream check box, as shown in Figure 8.3, to use Photo Stream on your Mac.**

7. **Select the Shared Photo Streams check box if you want to create shared photo streams or view streams that others create.**

Photo Stream Options

☑ My Photo Stream
Automatically download new photos from iCloud and upload photos you add to your photo stream from this computer.

☑ Shared Photo Streams
Create photo streams to share with other people, or subscribe to other people's shared photo streams.

Cancel   OK

8.3 In the Photo Stream Options dialog, select the My Photo Stream check box to use Photo Stream on your Mac.

8. **Click OK.** The Photo Stream Options dialog closes.

9. **Choose System Preferences ⇨ Quit System Preferences.** Alternatively, press ⌘+Q or click the red Close button at the left end of the window's title bar. System Preferences closes.

Setting up Photo Stream on a PC

To set up Photo Stream on your PC, you must first download and install Apple's iCloud Control Panel app — unless you've already installed it on your PC. You then use iCloud Control Panel to turn on Photo Stream.

Genius

If you think iCloud Control Panel may already be installed on your PC, choose Start ⇨ Control Panel. In the View by drop-down list, choose Large Icons. Then see if the iCloud icon appears. If so, click it to open iCloud Control Panel.

Here's how to download and install the iCloud Control Panel:

1. **Open your Web browser and go to www.apple.com/icloud/setup/pc.html.**

2. **Click the Download link to download the iCloudSetup.exe file to your PC.**

3. **When the download finishes, click Run.** The installer starts running and displays the Welcome to the iCloud Control Panel screen.

4. **Click Next.** The License Agreement screen appears.

5. **If you want to proceed, select the I agree to the terms of the license radio button, and then click Next.** The Installation Options screen appears.

6. **If you want to change the folder in which Windows installs the iCloud Control Panel, click Change (see Figure 8.4), select the folder on the Change Current Destination Folder screen, and then click OK.** Otherwise, leave the installation set to the default folder.

7. **Click Install.** Windows displays the User Account Control dialog box shown in Figure 8.5 to confirm that you want to install the software.

8. **Click Yes.** The installation runs, and then the Welcome to iCloud screen appears.

9. **Select the Open the iCloud Control Panel check box, as shown in Figure 8.6, if you want to open the iCloud Control Panel automatically.**

8.4 On the Installation Options screen, you can choose to install the iCloud Control Panel in a different folder. Normally, the default folder is a good choice.

8.5 The User Account Control dialog box asks you to confirm the software installation.

iCloud Control Panel 2.0

Welcome to iCloud

The iCloud Control Panel 2.0 has been installed on your computer.

Use the Windows Control Panel to open iCloud and manage your settings.

☑ Open the iCloud Control Panel   < Back   Finish   Cancel

8.6 On the Welcome to iCloud screen, select the Open the iCloud Control Panel check box.

10. **Click Finish.** The installer closes, and (assuming that you selected the check box) the iCloud Control Panel opens.

Note The installer for iCloud Control Panel may cause Windows to display more than one User Account Control dialog box. If so, verify that each is asking about software you want to install, and then click Yes to proceed.

With the iCloud Control Panel installed on your PC, follow these steps to turn on Photo Stream:

1. **Open the iCloud Control Panel.** If you just installed the iCloud Control Panel and allowed the installer to start the applet, you're set. Otherwise, perform the following steps to start it:

   - **Choose Start ⇨ Control Panel.** A Control Panel window opens.

   - **In the View by drop-down list, choose Large Icons.**

   - **Click iCloud.** The iCloud Control Panel opens and displays the iCloud dialog box.

2. **Type your Apple ID and password, as shown in Figure 8.7.**

```
 iCloud                                                          [-][□][X]
                                                                     2.0

                    iCloud stores your content and wirelessly pushes it to your devices.

                    Sign in with your Apple ID:

   [cloud icon]     jane_apfelfresser@me.com        ●●●●●●

   iCloud           Forgot Apple ID or password?

   [Learn more about iCloud...]              [ Sign in ]   [ Cancel ]
```

8.7 In the iCloud dialog box, type your Apple ID and password.

3. **Click Sign in.** The Terms of Service dialog box appears.

4. **Select the I have read and agree to the iCloud Terms of Service check box if you want to proceed.**

5. **Click Continue.** The iCloud Control Panel appears.

6. **Select the Photo Stream check box, as shown in Figure 8.8.** Select the check box for any other feature that you want to use.

7. **Click Options on the right side of the Photo Stream box.** The Photo Stream Options dialog box opens.

8.8 In the iCloud Control Panel, select the Photo Stream check box to turn on Photo Stream for your PC.

8. **Select the My Photo Stream check box, as shown in Figure 8.9, to add the PC to your photo stream.**

9. **Select the Shared Photo Streams check box if you want to share your photo streams or view those created by others.**

10. **If you want to change the folder iCloud uses for your Photo Stream folders, click Change, select the folder in the Browse For Folder dialog box that opens, and then click OK.** Otherwise, simply note the default folder — a Photo Stream folder in the Pictures folder under your user account.

11. **Click OK.** The Photo Stream Options dialog box closes.

12. **Click Apply.**

13. **Click Close.** The iCloud Control Panel closes and applies the settings that you chose.

8.9 In the Photo Stream Options dialog box, you normally want to select the My Photo Stream check box.

Note

If you selected the Mail, Contacts, Calendars, & Tasks with Outlook check box in the iCloud Control Panel, the Outlook Setup for iCloud dialog box appears after you click Apply in the iCloud Control Panel. Follow through the prompts to set up Outlook with iCloud.

Setting up Photo Stream on your iOS device

If you have an iPad, iPhone, or iPod touch, you can set up Photo Stream on it to sync your latest photos with your compass and your Apple TV. Photo Stream automatically uploads the photos you take on your iOS device and downloads the photos you've added using your computer.

Here's how to set up Photo Stream on your iPad, iPhone, or iPod touch:

1. **Press the Home button.** The Home screen appears.

2. **Tap Settings.** The Settings screen appears.

3. **Tap Photos & Camera.** The Photos & Camera screen appears.

4. **Tap the My Photo Stream switch and move it to the On position, as shown in Figure 8.10.** This screen is from the iPad; the iPhone and iPod touch versions have the same controls.

5. **If you want to use Shared Photo Streams, tap the Shared Photo Streams switch and move it to the On position.**

8.10 On the Photos & Camera screen, move the My Photo Stream switch to the On position.

Note

If you have not yet signed into iCloud when you go to turn on Photo Stream, your iPad prompts you to sign into iCloud.

Setting up Photo Stream on your Apple TV

When you have set up Photo Stream on the computers and devices that will provide the photos, you can set up Photo Stream on your Apple TV and access the photos.

Follow these steps to set up Photo Stream on your Apple TV:

1. **If the Home screen isn't currently displayed, press the Menu button one or more times until it appears.**

2. **Select Photo Stream.** The Photo Stream Setup screen appears.

Note If you haven't yet set up your iCloud account on your Apple TV, the Photo Stream app displays the Account Name screen without showing the Photo Stream Setup screen.

3. **If you want to use the iCloud account you've already set up on your Apple TV, select Yes, as shown in Figure 8.11.** Otherwise, perform the following actions:

   - **Select No, use a different account.** The Account Name screen appears.

   - **Type the account name, and then select Submit.** The Password screen appears.

   - **Type your password, and then select Submit.**

Photo Stream Setup

Would you like to turn on Photo Stream using the account
jane_apfelfresser@me.com?

Yes

No, use a different account

8.11 On the Photo Stream Setup screen, select Yes if you want to use the iCloud account that is already set up on your Apple TV.

4. **On the Use Photo Stream as Screen Saver Screen, shown in Figure 8.12, select Yes or No, as appropriate.**

Use Photo Stream as Screen Saver?

Would you like to use Photo Stream as your screen saver?

Yes

No

8.12 Choose whether to use Photo Stream as your screen saver.

You can now start viewing your photos as discussed in the next section.

Caution Using Photo Stream as your screen saver can increase usage of your Internet connection. So if your connection is running full bore to service your home, you probably don't want to use Photo Stream as your screen saver. The Apple TV does cache some of your Photo Stream photos, but it doesn't normally have space to cache all of them — and in any case, it checks frequently for new photos in your Photo Stream.

Viewing Photos with Photo Stream

After you set up Photo Stream as described in the previous section, you can view your photos on the TV or monitor connected to your Apple TV. To start viewing your photos in Photo Stream, choose Photo Stream from the Apple TV Home screen. Your Photo Stream screen appears (see Figure 8.13). From here, you can browse photos, start a slide show, or choose custom slide show settings.

8.13 Choose Photo Stream from the Apple TV Home screen to open your Photo Stream.

Browsing individual photos

To browse individual photos, press the Up, Down, Left, or Right buttons as needed to highlight a photo, and then press the Select button to display it full screen. From here, follow these instructions to navigate your Photo Stream:

- **Display the previous photo.** Press the Left button.

- **Display the next photo.** Press the Right button.

- **Start a slide show.** Press the Play/Pause button.

- **Return to your Photo Stream screen.** Press the Menu button.

Viewing a slide show

To start a slide show with all the photos in your Photo Stream, press the Play/Pause button. To start a slide show from a particular photo, highlight that photo, and then press the Play/Pause button. The slide show starts playing using your current settings; see the next section if you want to change them.

When the slide show is running, you can control it in the following ways:

- **Pause or resume the slide show.** Press the Play/Pause button.
- **Display the previous photo.** Press the Left button.
- **Display the next photo.** Press the Right button.
- **End the slide show.** Press the Menu button.

Choosing slide show settings

To control how your slide show plays, choose Settings from your Photo Stream screen. You can then choose the following settings on the Settings screen:

- **Shuffle Photos.** Select this option, as shown in Figure 8.14, to toggle the setting between Off (playing the photos in order) and On (playing the photos in random order).

- **Repeat Photos.** Select this option to toggle the setting between Off (no repeating) and On (repeating when you reach the end).

- **Default Music.** Selecting this option displays the Default Music screen. You can then select the library to use as the default for music. Select None if you prefer peace.

- **Shuffle Music.** This option toggles the setting between Off (the music plays in order) and On (the music plays in random order).

- **Themes.** Select a theme to use for the slide show. When you highlight one, your Apple TV displays a preview of it.

Slideshow Settings

Shuffle Photos	Off
Repeat Photos	Off
Default Music	>
Shuffle Music	On
Themes	
Random	
Flip-up	
Holiday Mobile	
Origami	
Photo Mobile	
Photo Wall	

8.14 Use the Settings screen to set up your slide show.

If you select the Ken Burns theme or the Classic theme, choose options on the screen that appears. Figure 8.15 shows the Ken Burns screen (the Classic screen has the same controls). From here, you can choose the time per slide and the transition effect that you want to use.

Ken Burns

Time Per Slide   3 seconds

Transitions

Random

Cube

✓ Dissolve

Droplet

Fade Through Black

Fade Through White

Flip

Move In

Page Flip

8.15 On the Ken Burns screen, choose the time per slide and transition effect for the slide show.

These are the options on both the Ken Burns and Classic screens:

- **Highlight Time Per Slide, and then press the Select button one or more times to set the number of seconds to play each slide.** Your choices are 2 seconds, 3 seconds, 5 seconds, 10 seconds, and 20 seconds.

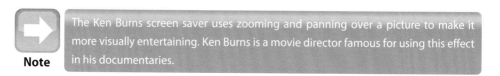

Note The Ken Burns screen saver uses zooming and panning over a picture to make it more visually entertaining. Ken Burns is a movie director famous for using this effect in his documentaries.

- **In the Transitions list, select the transition that you want to use.** The Dissolve transition is the most discreet; others, such as Cube and Flip, are more in-your-face.

- **Press the Menu button to return to the Screen Saver screen.**

Clearing Photo Stream Images from the Apple TV

Sometimes you may decide to clear out your old photos from Photo Stream. You can do this by deleting the photos from Photo Stream on the Apple TV (as covered in this chapter), or on your computer or iOS device.

If you delete the photos using your computer or iOS device, some of the deleted photos will likely remain in your Apple TV's cache for a while before being deleted. So when you browse your Photo Stream on your Apple TV, you may see the photos you have deleted elsewhere. Similarly, if you use Photo Stream as your Apple TV's screen saver, you may see deleted photos there. If you want to clear out the old photos to make sure they don't appear, choose Sign Out from the main Photo Stream screen. Your Apple TV then clears all photos from the cache.

Deleting a photo from Photo Stream

Photo Stream can be wonderful, but if you take indiscreet or highly personal photos, you may not want them to appear in Photo Stream. To delete a photo from Photo Stream on the Apple TV, highlight the photo, and then hold down the Select button. When the dialog shown in Figure 8.16 appears, select Delete Photo.

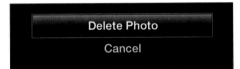

8.16 You can delete a photo from Photo Stream on the Apple TV.

Browsing Photos on Flickr

Photo Stream is great for your recent photos, but you may also want to browse other photos. You can also use your Apple TV to connect to the Flickr service to browse photos on there. If you have a Flickr account, you can upload your photos so you can easily browse them on your Apple TV. You can also browse photos that other Flickr users share with the public.

Genius

On Flickr, you can keep your photos private; share them with friends, family, or both; or share them with the public. Because your Apple TV doesn't log into a Flickr account, it can access only photos shared with the public. So if you want to view your own Flickr photos on your Apple TV, you must share them with the public.

Adding a Flickr contact

Before you can browse a Flickr contact's photos, you must help your Apple TV identify the contact. You can do so by either typing the contact's Flickr name (if you know it) or by searching for the name. To get started, select Flickr from the Apple TV Home screen. The Flickr screen appears, as shown in Figure 8.17.

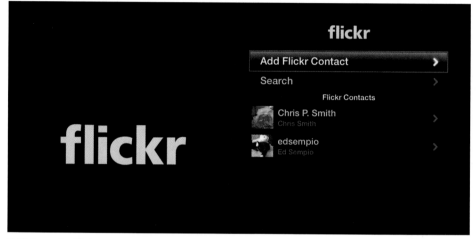

8.17 From the Flickr screen, you can add a Flickr contact.

Note The Flickr Contacts list appears on the Flickr screen only after you add a contact.

Adding a contact by name

If you know the Flickr contact's name, you can quickly add the contact to your Flickr list. This is the technique you'll use when adding your own Flickr account.

Follow these steps to add a Flickr contact by name:

1. **From the Flickr screen, select Add Flickr Contact.** The Add Flickr Contact screen appears, as shown in Figure 8.18.

2. **Type the contact's Flickr name.**

8.18 Use the Add Flickr Contact screen to add a contact.

3. **Select Submit.** The Flickr app verifies the name, and then adds the contact's name to the Flickr screen.

Genius

After adding a contact, you can browse that contact's contact list and add contacts from there to your own contacts list. In your Flickr Contacts list, select the contact to display the contact's Flickr screen. From there, select the Contacts item to display the Contacts list. You can then select a contact and select the Add item to add the contact to your list.

Searching for a contact

If you don't know a contact's Flickr name, you may be able to add that person by searching.

Caution

At this writing, the Flickr search feature is hit or miss. Instead of returning a list of results from which you can pick the most likely match, the search feature either displays the apparent best match or announces that it found no matches. The apparent best match may be completely different from what you're looking for, so explore it with care.

Follow these steps to search for a contact:

1. **From the Flickr screen, select Search.** The Flickr Search screen appears.

2. **Type the contact's name or another search term, such as an identifying keyword or company name.**

3. **Select Submit.** The Flickr app searches and returns either a match, or a message saying that there was no match.

Browsing a contact's albums and viewing slide shows

After adding a contact, you can browse the contact's albums. In your Flickr Contacts list, select the contact to display that person's screen, as shown in Figure 8.19, and then select the album that you want to view.

8.19 On a contact's screen, select the album that you want to view.

From an album's screen (see Figure 8.20), you can view the photos in the following ways:

- **Browse.** Press the Up, Down, Left, or Right buttons to highlight the photo that you want to view, and then press the Select button to display it. You can then press the Right button to display the next photo, the Left button to display the previous photo, or the Play/Pause button to start a slide show from that photo.

8.20 From an album's screen, you can browse the photos or start a slide show.

- **Start a slide show.** At the top of the album's screen, select Slideshow.

Genius

The Flickr app offers the same slide-show options as Photo Stream (discussed earlier in this chapter). So, if you've chosen settings that you like in Photo Stream, the Flickr app picks them up automatically. To change the settings, select Settings at the top of an album's screen, and then work on the screen that appears.

How Do I Set Up and Use a Remote Control?

Your Apple TV comes with a sleek remote control that enables you to navigate its user interface easily. The Apple Remote usually needs no further maintenance than the occasional battery replacement. However, you can also use your preferred universal remote to control your Apple TV, which might give you dedicated buttons for actions, such as skipping ahead or back, that the Apple Remote doesn't offer. You can also turn your iPhone, iPod touch, or iPad into a remote, and control your Apple TV from a device that you always have with you.

Replacing the Battery in the Apple Remote Control 176

Using a Different Remote Control with your Apple TV 176

Using an iOS Device as a Remote Control 183

Replacing the Battery in the Apple Remote Control

If the battery in your Apple Remote runs out, you can follow these steps to easily replace it:

1. **Buy a replacement CR2032 battery.** This is a standard battery used in computers and electronic devices. It is about the size of a U.S. quarter.

Genius You can buy a single CR2032 battery from any electrical store, but you can usually get a much better deal by buying a strip of five or 10 batteries from an online retailer, such as Amazon or eBay.

2. **Unscrew the back of the Apple Remote using a small coin or medium screwdriver.**
3. **Put the battery in with the plus side (+) facing you.**
4. **Screw the back of the remote back on.**

Note If you lose or damage your Apple Remote, you can buy another from the Apple Store (http://store.apple.com) or an online retailer, such as Amazon or Best Buy. At this writing, the Apple Remote costs around $19.

Using a Different Remote Control with Your Apple TV

The Apple Remote works well, but you may want to try using a different remote with your Apple TV. Using a different remote offers several advantages:

- **Simplicity.** You can control your Apple TV with the same remote control that you use for other devices. This means that you don't have to switch remotes in midstream.

- **Easier control.** You can teach your Apple TV to respond to buttons beyond the six that the Apple Remote offers. Extra buttons can make playback easier. For example, you can dedicate a button to skip ahead or return to the beginning of an item.

- **Handiness.** If you have large hands, you may find a larger remote easier to use — even if it has many more buttons.

Choosing a suitable remote for the Apple TV

The first step toward using a different remote is to get one. The Apple TV is pretty compatible with other remotes and works with many different kinds. If you already have a universal remote, chances are that you can get the Apple TV to respond to it. Similarly, if you already have an extra remote, it's worth trying that remote before buying a new one. If you want to use a universal remote, make sure that it has a device setting free. If you choose a single-device remote, use one that you're not using with any other device.

Genius

Another option is to use an existing remote that has extra buttons you're not using for your current remote-control setup. You can map those buttons to control the Apple TV. Doing this enables you to control both your existing devices and your Apple TV from the same remote control — but it may mean using awkwardly placed or little-used buttons on the remote for the Apple TV.

Configuring a remote for use with the Apple TV

Once you've gotten your remote, follow these steps to set it up with your Apple TV:

1. **From the Home screen, select Settings.** The Settings screen appears.

2. **Select General.** The General screen appears.

3. **Select Remotes.** The Remotes screen appears, as shown in Figure 9.1.

Remotes

Pair Apple Remote

Remote App   >

Learn Remote   >

To control Apple TV with another remote, you
need a remote that can control multiple
devices, or an unused single-device remote.

9.1 The Remotes screen is where you begin configuring your Apple TV to work with a third-party remote.

4. **Select Learn Remote.** The first Learn Remote screen appears, as shown in Figure 9.2.

Learn Remote

Before you start, choose an unused device setting on your other remote. Then select Start using your Apple TV remote.

Start

Cancel

9.2 On the first Learn Remote screen, use your Apple Remote to select Start.

5. **If you're adding a universal remote, choose an unused device setting on it.** If you're setting up a single-purpose remote that will be dedicated to the Apple TV, you don't need to change anything.

6. **Using your Apple Remote, select Start.** The second Learn Remote screen appears, as shown in Figure 9.3.

7. **Press and hold the Up button on the third-party remote until the blue progress bar on the Apple TV advances all of the way to the right.**

Genius

If you're setting up a straightforward mapping, press the matching buttons on the third-party remote — for example, map the Up button to the Up command. However, if you're setting up unused buttons on an otherwise busy remote, press the buttons that you want to use, no matter what function the remote intends them to have. For example, you can map the Subtitles button on the remote to the Up command if you want.

8. **Follow the training routine until you have taught your Apple TV all of the standard buttons.** The Remote Control Name screen then appears.

9. **Type the name that you want to give the remote, as shown in Figure 9.4.**

Learn Remote

Press and hold the Up button on the other remote.

Continue to hold the Up button until the progress bar is full.

SELECT   MENU

9.3 On the second Learn Remote screen, press each button in turn, following the prompts on screen.

Remote Control Name

| abc | ABC | #+= | Recent |

a	b	c	d	e	f
g	h	i	j	k	l
m	n	o	p	q	r
s	t	u	v	w	x
y	z	1	2	3	4
5	6	7	8	9	0

. _ @ .com .net .edu

SPACE   DELETE   CLEAR

Press ▶ II to change keyboards

Name:

Gray Giant Commander

Submit

9.4 On the Remote Control Name screen, type a name for the remote control.

10. **Select Submit.** The Setup Complete screen appears, as shown in Figure 9.5. If you're done setting up the remote, select OK and skip the remaining steps.

9.5 On the Setup Complete screen, you can select OK if you don't want to set up extra buttons on the remote.

11. **If you want to set up extra buttons on the remote to control playback, select Set Up Playback Buttons.** The Learn Remote screen then appears, as shown in Figure 9.6.

9.6 On the Learn Remote screen, set up the playback buttons that you want to use on the remote control.

12. **Press and hold the Play button on the third-party remote until the blue progress bar on the Apple TV advances all of the way to the right.**

13. **Follow through the training process by pressing and holding each button until you have configured all of those that you want to use for playback on your Apple TV.** The same as before, these buttons can be intended for such functions or those that you prefer to use.

Note   If you press a button you've already assigned to a different function, the Apple TV displays the Button Already Learned screen as a warning. Select Try Again to go back and assign another button. When on the screen for assigning buttons, you can press Left to go back to an earlier button in the sequence and start reassigning buttons from there on.

14. **When you reach the end of the training, the Remotes screen appears again, and now includes the remote that you added in the Other Remotes list, as shown in Figure 9.7.** Press the Menu button to return to the General screen, and then press it again to return to the Home screen.

9.7 Any remotes that you add appear in the Other Remotes list on the Remotes screen.

Renaming, reconfiguring, or deleting a remote

If you're happy with the way you set up the third-party remote, you can simply use it to control your Apple TV. If you want to rename a remote, reconfigure which button does what, or if you no longer want to use it, follow these steps:

1. **From the Home screen, select Settings.** The Settings screen appears.

2. **Select General.** The General screen appears.

3. **Select Remotes.** The Remotes screen appears.

4. **In the Other Remotes list, select the remote that you want to change.** The screen for that remote appears, as shown in Figure 9.8.

Gray Giant Commander Remote

Rename Remote

Delete Remote

Set Up Basic Buttons

Set Up Playback Buttons

9.8 On the screen for the remote, choose which action that you want to change.

5. **Select one of the following actions:**

- **Rename Remote.** Select this to display the Remote Control Name screen. Type the new name for the remote, and then select Submit.

- **Delete Remote.** Select this option to stop the remote from controlling your Apple TV. On the confirmation screen that appears, select Delete, as shown in Figure 9.9.

Are you sure you want to delete "Gray Giant Commander Remote" from your Apple TV?

Cancel

Delete

9.9 On this confirmation screen, select Delete to stop using the remote to control your Apple TV.

- **Set Up Basic Buttons.** Select this to go through the sequence of assigning actions to the basic buttons: Left, Right, Up, Down, Select, and Play/Pause.

- **Set Up Playback Buttons.** Select this option to go through the sequence of assigning playback actions: Play, Pause, Stop, Rewind, Fast/Forward, and so on.

Using an iOS Device as a Remote Control

If you have an iPhone, iPod touch, or iPad, you can use it not only as your satellite source for music, video, and other entertainment but also as a remote control for your Apple TV. To use your iOS device as a remote control, you download, install, and run the free app called Remote. You can download and install the Remote app using either your iOS device or iTunes on your computer.

Downloading and installing the Remote app using an iOS device

Here's how to download and install the Remote app using your iPhone, iPod touch, or iPad:

1. **Press Home.** The Home screen appears.

2. **Tap App Store.** The App Store app opens.

3. **On the iPhone or iPod touch, tap Search.** The Search screen appears. On the iPad, tap in the Search field.

4. **Type remote, and then tap Search.**

5. **Tap Free.** The Install button appears.

6. **Tap Install or Install App.** iOS downloads and installs the app.

7. **Tap Open.** The Remote app opens.

Downloading and installing the Remote app using iTunes

Here's how to download and install the Remote app using iTunes:

1. **Double-click iTunes Store in the Store category in the Source list.** A separate window opens showing the iTunes Store.

2. **Click App Store in the tab bar at the top.**

3. **Click in the Search Store box in the upper-right corner.**

4. **Type remote, and then press Enter or Return.** A list of results appears.

5. **Click the Free button on the Remote app in the iPhone Apps list (for an iPhone or iPod touch) or on the Remote app in the iPad Apps list (for an iPad).**

183

6. **If the Sign In to download from the iTunes Store dialog appears, type your pass-word, and then click Get.**

7. **After iTunes downloads the app, connect your iOS device to your computer either wirelessly or using the USB cable, and then click Sync to perform a sync.**

Controlling the Apple TV with the Remote app

After installing the Remote app on your iOS device, launch the app by tapping its icon on the Home screen. This section shows the Remote app running on the iPhone. The user interface on the iPod touch looks almost the same, and the user interface on the iPad is very similar.

If you haven't yet turned on Home Sharing on your iOS device, the Remote app prompts you to do so, as shown in Figure 9.10. Tap the Home Sharing button, type your Apple ID and password on the Home Sharing screen, as shown in Figure 9.11, and then tap Done.

9.10 The opening screen of the Remote app prompts you to turn on Home Sharing if you haven't already done so.

9.11 On the Home Sharing screen, type your Apple ID and password, and then tap Done.

Next, you see the Home Sharing screen shown in Figure 9.12, which tells you that Home Sharing is on, and provides brief instructions for controlling iTunes and the Apple TV. Tap Done. The Remote screen shown in Figure 9.13 then appears.

9.12 When you see this Home Sharing screen, tap Done.

9.13 On the Remote screen, tap the Apple TV that you want to control.

Tap your Apple TV to display the items that you can play on it, as shown in Figure 9.14. Tap Control in the toolbar to display the Control screen. You can then control your Apple TV by taking the following actions:

- **Drag left, right, up, or down to move the highlight on the TV or monitor connected to the Apple TV.**
- **Tap to select the highlighted item.**
- **Tap Menu to give the Menu command on the Apple TV.** For example, you may need to tap Menu several times to go up the menu structure to the Home screen.
- **Tap the Options button, shown in Figure 9.15, to display a list of available options.** For example, when playing a song, tap the Options button to display the dialog that gives the choices Start Genius, Browse Artist, Browse Album, and Cancel.
- **Tap the Play/Pause button to start, pause, or resume playback.**

Tap Done when you finish using your iOS device as a remote control.

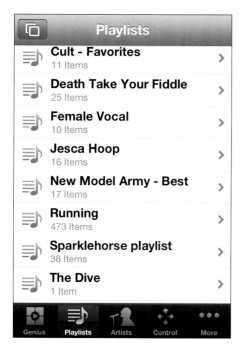

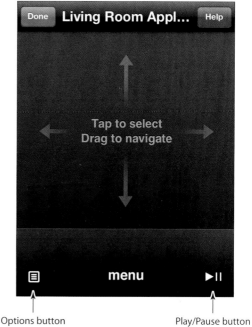

Options button   Play/Pause button

9.14 After connecting to your Apple TV, tap Control in the toolbar at the bottom of the screen.

9.15 In Control mode, you can control your Apple TV from your iOS device.

What Can I Do with the WSJ Live App?

The WSJ Live app included with your Apple TV gives you access to video content from the *Wall Street Journal*. Using the WSJ Live app, you can watch live broadcasts on the WSJ channel, including the latest news on markets and technology. You can also watch programs from the *Wall Street Journal's* extensive video archive, which is great for education, research, and general interest. To find programs that you're interested in, you can browse through the schedule, look through specific categories of videos, or search keywords.

Opening the WSJ Live App 190

Watching Live Broadcasts 190

Finding Programs 190

Opening the WSJ Live App

To open the WSJ Live app, go to the Apple TV home screen, and then select WSJ Live. When the app opens, you see the WSJ Live screen (shown on the opening page of this chapter). From here, you can access the following five areas of the WSJ Live app:

- **Watch Live Now.** Select this item to watch live broadcasts.
- **Schedule.** Select this item to browse the schedule.
- **All Videos.** Select this item to browse the entire video library.
- **Videos by Category.** Select this item to browse videos by categories, such as U.S., World, Business, and Markets.
- **Search.** Select this item to search by keyword for subjects that interest you.

Watching Live Broadcasts

To catch up with the latest news, select Watch Live Now from the WSJ Live Home screen. You then see the current live broadcast, much as if you were watching TV. You can pause playback by pressing the Play/Pause button on the Apple Remote. To resume playback, press the Play/Pause button again.

Note

At this writing, live broadcasts start at 6:30 a.m. Eastern Time. If it's earlier than this, you see a message telling you to wait until 6:30 a.m.

Finding Programs

When the live broadcasts don't appeal to you, you can find programs that you want to watch by browsing the schedule or the full list of programs. You can also browse by categories, or search for terms or keywords. In the following sections, I explain how to use each of these methods to find programs.

Browsing the schedule

To identify upcoming programs that you want to watch, follow these steps to browse the schedule:

1. **From the WSJ Live Home screen, select Schedule.** The Schedule screen appears, showing the schedule for the day, as shown in Figure 10.1.

10.1 Browsing the schedule lets you find upcoming programs that you want to watch.

2. **Scroll down the schedule to see additional programs.**

3. **To see the schedule for a different day, press the Right or Left button, as appropriate.** For example, from the Today schedule, press the Left button to see the schedule for the previous day. Press the Left button again to go further back in time. Figure 10.2 shows an example of the Yesterday schedule screen.

10.2 Press the Left button to go back to previous days and catch up on programs that you missed.

4. **To view details about a program, select it.** The summary screen appears, as shown in Figure 10.3.

5. **To watch a program that has already been broadcast, select Play on its summary screen.** The program starts playing.

10.3 Use the summary screen to decide whether to watch a program.

Browsing the full list

When you want to see the entire range of content available in the WSJ Live app, select the All Videos category. Your Apple TV then displays the All Videos list, as shown in Figure 10.4.

From here, select the show or topic you want to view. On the summary screen for the show, select Play if you want to play the video, as shown in Figure 10.5, or press the Menu button to return to the All Videos list so you can browse further.

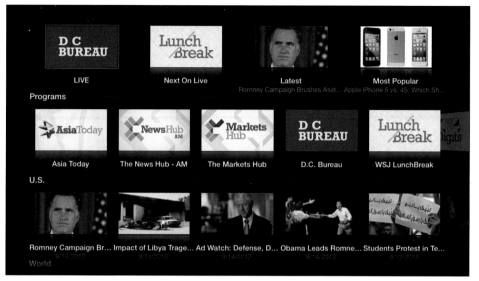

10.4 Browse the All Videos list when you want to get an overview of all of the content available on WSJ Live.

10.5 From the Summary screen for a show, select Play to start the video.

Browsing by category

When you know the type of programs you want to view, the best way to browse is by categories. Categories enable you to zero in on the topics you want without having to look at other topics. At this writing, the following categories are included in the WSJ Live app:

- **U.S.** This category contains general news focused on the United States.

- **World.** This category contains international news.

- **Business.** This category covers business news (with the exception of tech and personal finance news, which are covered in the Tech and Personal Finance categories).

- **Markets.** This category focuses on stock market news.

- **Opinion.** This category presents opinion pieces about newsworthy topics.

- **Tech.** This category contains news stories about technology.

- **Life & Culture.** This category covers lifestyle and culture topics — everything from football (American and soccer), to fashion and royalty.

- **Personal Finance.** This category presents stories about personal finance, property, and similar topics.

- **Most Popular.** This category draws together the most popular stories from all of the other categories. It's a good place to find out about the day's hottest topics.

Follow these steps to browse by categories:

1. **From the WSJ Live Home screen, select Videos by Category.** The Videos by Category screen appears, as shown in Figure 10.6.

10.6 On the Videos by Category screen, select the category that you want to browse.

2. **Select the category that you want to browse, and that screen appears.** For example, if you select Tech, that category's screen appears, as shown in Figure 10.7.

10.7 When you select a category, its screen appears.

3. **Select the video that you want to view.** The video's summary screen appears, as shown in Figure 10.8.

4. **Select Play if you want to play the video.** Otherwise, press the Menu button to return to the category screen and browse further.

10.8 After you select the video that you want to watch, its summary screen appears.

Searching for programs

As you've seen in the previous sections, browsing can be a great way to find programs you want to watch. But when you need to focus in on a particular interest, you'll usually do better by searching.

Here's how to search for programs using keywords:

1. **From the WSJ Live Home screen, select Search.** The Search screen appears.

2. **Type your search term, or just the beginning of it.** The Search screen displays matching items, as shown in Figure 10.9.

10.9 On the Search screen, type your search term.

3. **Scroll the search results to see more if you don't see the item that you want to watch.**

4. **If necessary, type further search terms or keywords to refine the search results.** As you type, the WSJ Live app searches and displays matching items.

5. **Select the search result that you want to see.** The WSJ Live app displays its summary screen, as shown in Figure 10.10.

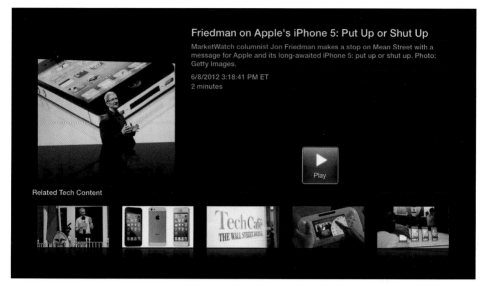

10.10 Click on an item in the search results to go to its summary screen.

6. **Select Play to play the item, or press the Menu button on the remote to return to the Search screen and browse other results, or change your search term.**

Genius

When searching using various search terms, use the Recent keyboard to quickly enter search terms you've used before.

How Can I Add More Capabilities to My Apple TV?

Your Apple TV comes with great built-in capabilities — but what if you want it to do even more? In this chapter, I cover several extra features you may want to add. First, you can use third-party apps to send movies from your Mac to your Apple TV, which is useful if you have movies that iTunes can't play. Second, you can mirror your Mac or PC on your Apple TV. Third, I explain what jailbreaking is and briefly discusses the extra features that you can add with the third-party aTV Flash software.

Sending Movies to Your Apple TV 200

Mirroring Your Computer on Your Apple TV with AirParrot.........202

Understanding Jailbreaking......................................206

Adding Capabilities with aTV Flash 207

Sending Movies to Your Apple TV

As you've seen earlier in this book, your Apple TV can play movies shared using Home Sharing in iTunes. You can also stream movies from iTunes or from your iOS device to your Apple TV. iTunes supports a good variety of movie formats, but if you take your own videos or download files from the Internet, you likely have files in formats iTunes doesn't play. In this case, you can convert the movies to iTunes-friendly formats — but you may prefer to try Beamer instead.

Beamer (http://beamer-app.com) is an app that streams movies from your Mac to your Apple TV. Beamer can play a wide variety of movie formats, including AVI, WMV, and FLV. Beamer costs $15 for a license, but there's a free trial version that's limited to playing the first 15 minutes of any file, so you can easily make sure Beamer can handle the files you want to play.

After you download Beamer, unzip the distribution file, and then drag the Beamer file to your Applications folder. You can then run Beamer by clicking the Launchpad icon on the Dock, typing b, and then clicking the Beamer icon on the Launchpad screen. If your network has two or more Apple TVs, as shown in Figure 11.1, click the button for the one that you want to use.

11.1 If Beamer displays this screen, click the Apple TV to which you want to stream video.

Genius

If you like, you can run Beamer from the folder into which you unzipped it. If you want the app to appear on the Launchpad screen and be available to others using your Mac, drag it to the Applications folder.

When Beamer knows which Apple TV to use, it displays the main Beamer window. To open a movie, either drag it from a Finder window, as shown in Figure 11.2, or choose File ⇨ Open, select the file in the Open dialog, and then click Open.

11.2 The quickest way to open a movie file is to drag it from a Finder window to the Beamer window.

Note

If you have multiple Apple TVs, you can switch among them using the Connected to pop-up menu at the bottom of the Beamer window.

Beamer opens the movie file that you chose, connects to the Apple TV, and then plays the file, as shown in Figure 11.3. After playback starts, you can control it either with the Apple TV remote control or the Play/Pause button in the Beamer window. When you finish using Beamer, press ⌘+Q or choose Beamer ⇨ Quit Beamer.

11.3 Beamer streams the video file to your Apple TV.

201

Mirroring Your Computer on Your Apple TV with AirParrot

AirParrot lets you mirror your PC's screen or Mac's screen on your Apple TV. This can be great for a wide range of activities, such as sharing photos, giving presentations, or collaborating on documents. AirParrot runs on OS X versions 10.6.8 or later, so it'll work as long as your Mac has Snow Leopard, Lion, or Mountain Lion. On PCs, AirParrot works with Windows XP and later versions — Windows Vista, Windows 7, and Windows 8.

AirParrot on the Mac provides several more features than AirParrot on Windows, allowing you to use your Apple TV's display as an extension of your Mac's desktop and letting you mirror a specific application instead of your entire desktop. This section shows AirParrot running on the Mac and notes the main differences in the Windows version.

To get AirParrot, take your computer's browser to the AirParrot website (http://airparrot.com). AirParrot costs $9.99 for a single-seat license or $29.99 for a five-seat license, but normally it's a good idea to first download the time-limited free trial to see if you like AirParrot well enough to pay for it. Download, install, and run AirParrot as explained in the following sections.

Working with AirParrot on a Mac

To download AirParrot on a Mac, click the Download button on the AirParrot website. If your Mac doesn't open a Finder window showing the contents of the disk image file you downloaded, click Downloads on the Dock, then click the AirParrot disk image. In the Finder window, drag AirParrot to the Applications folder. You can now run AirParrot by clicking the Launchpad icon on the Dock, typing *a* (or *air*), and then clicking the AirParrot icon.

Genius

If you want AirParrot to launch automatically when you log in, choose Apple ⟳ System Preferences, and then choose View ⟳ Users & Groups to display the Users & Groups pane. With your user account selected in the left box, click Login Items to display the Login Items tab. Click Add (+), click Applications, click AirParrot, and then click Add.

On a Mac, AirParrot appears as a menu on the menu bar. Click the icon to display the menu, as shown in Figure 11.4.

To get full AirParrot functionality on your Mac, including the desktop-extension feature, follow these steps to install a display driver:

1. **Save and close any open documents.** The installation procedure has to restart your Mac.

2. **Click the AirParrot icon, and then click Extend Desktop.** AirParrot displays the AirParrot Driver Not Found dialog, shown in Figure 11.5.

3. **Click OK.** The Authentication dialog appears.

4. **Type your password, and then press Return.** The Restart Needed dialog appears.

5. **Click Restart.** Your Mac restarts and the installation completes.

11.4 Click the AirParrot icon on the OS X menu bar to open the AirParrot menu.

11.5 The AirParrot Driver Not Found dialog asks you to confirm if you would like to install the display driver.

Working with AirParrot on a PC

To download AirParrot on a Windows PC, click the Download button on the AirParrot website. When your browser prompts you to run the downloaded file, click Run. The AirParrot Setup Wizard opens. Follow through the Wizard's screens to complete the installation. As usual, you must accept the license agreement, and then click Yes in the User Account Control dialog box that Windows displays to confirm that you intend to install the software.

Note If the AirParrot icon doesn't appear in the notification area, click the Show Hidden Icons button (the button showing an upward-pointing arrow) at the left end of the notification area to display the hidden icons.

After installing AirParrot, you run it by clicking the Start button, and then clicking the AirParrot icon. If a Windows Security Alert dialog box appears the first time that you run AirParrot, as shown in Figure 11.6, select the Private networks, such as my home or work network check box, and then click Allow access.

11.6 The Windows Security Alert dialog box may appear the first time that you run AirParrot.

After you start AirParrot, the program appears as an icon in the notification area at the right side of the taskbar. Right-click the icon, and then click the appropriate command on the menu, as shown in Figure 11.7.

Displaying your desktop on your Apple TV

AirParrot's main feature is to display your desktop on your Apple TV. This capability is great for lots of purposes, from giving instructions to collaborating on documents.

11.7 Right-click the AirParrot icon in the Windows notification area to display the AirParrot menu.

To display your desktop, open the AirParrot menu, and then click the Apple TV on which you want to display it. A check mark then appears next to the Apple TV on the menu. To stop displaying the desktop, open the menu again, and then click the Apple TV entry again to remove the check mark.

Genius

If your Mac is running OS X Mountain Lion, you can use the AirPlay Mirroring feature to display your desktop on your Apple TV.

Displaying a single app on your Apple TV

If you're running AirParrot on a Mac, you can display a single app on your Apple TV instead of displaying the whole desktop. This feature is useful when you need to demonstrate only a particular app or you have items on your desktop you don't want to share.

To display a single app, open the AirParrot menu, click Specific App, and then click the app on the submenu. AirParrot puts a check mark next to the app on the menu. To change the app, open the menu, click Specific App again, and then click the app to which you want to switch. To stop displaying the current app, open the menu, click Specific app, and then click the current app, removing its check mark.

Extending a Mac desktop to your Apple TV

AirParrot's other main feature for Macs is extending the desktop to the Apple TV. If the Apple TV's TV or monitor is near your Mac (or you position your Mac near the TV or monitor), this is a very useful feature for giving yourself more desktop real estate in which to work. To extend your Mac's desktop to your Apple TV, open the AirParrot menu, and then click Extend Desktop. AirParrot starts using the TV or monitor as an extra display, and you can position windows on it just as you would with a normal display.

To get the most out of the Apple TV as a desktop extension, follow these steps to ensure that your Mac knows where the Apple TV's monitor is positioned in relation to the Mac's monitor (or monitors):

1. **Choose Apple ⇨ System Preferences.** The System Preferences window opens.

2. **In the Hardware section, click Displays.** The Displays pane appears on each of your Mac's monitors.

3. **On your Mac's main monitor, click Arrangement in the tab bar at the top of the Displays pane.** The Arrangement pane appears, as shown in Figure 11.8.

11.8 Use the Arrangement pane in the Displays preferences to tell your Mac where the Apple TV monitor is positioned.

4. **If you're not sure which icon represents which display, click one.** The monitor shows a red line around its edges to identify it.

5. **Click and drag the icon for the Apple TV television or monitor to the appropriate position.**

6. **If you want to put the menu bar on the Apple TV monitor or television, click the white strip at the top of the display's icon, and then drag it to the other display's icon.**

7. **When you finish positioning the displays and the menu bar, choose System Preferences ⇨ Quit System Preferences.** System Preferences closes.

To turn off the desktop extension, open the AirParrot menu, and then click Extend Desktop again. This removes the check mark from the menu item.

Understanding Jailbreaking

If you want to get even more out of your Apple TV than is possible with the apps you've seen so far in this book, you can jailbreak your Apple TV and install unapproved third-party software on it. For example, you can install the popular aTV Flash software suite, discussed in the next section, to add capabilities ranging from playing DVDs and other media formats the Apple TV doesn't natively support to surfing the web and keeping up with blogs.

Out of the box, the Apple TV's software contains protective features that keep it within the ecosystem that Apple has designed and limit it to running software approved by Apple. This ecosystem is called a *walled garden* — a safe area protected from the wilds of the Internet. *Jailbreaking* involves installing a customized version of iOS that removes the protective features, allowing the Apple TV to go outside the walled garden.

Note This book doesn't show you how to jailbreak your Apple TV, but you can easily find instructions on the Internet. The technology changes rapidly, so before attempting a jailbreak, double-check that the instructions apply to the Apple TV model and version of iOS that you are using.

Adding Capabilities with aTV Flash

If you jailbreak your Apple TV, you may well want to install aTV Flash, a software suite from FireCore, LLC (http://firecore.com). At this writing, aTV Flash costs $29.95 and offers a wide range of extra capabilities, including the following:

● **Installing extra software.** You can customize your Apple TV by choosing which apps and packages to install (see Figure 11.9).

remotehd-atv2

Installing remotehd-atv2...

Get:4 http://apt.modmyi.com stable/main 2012-10-13-2054.05.pdiff [4219B]

Hit http://nitosoft.com Packages

Get:5 http://apt.modmyi.com stable/main 2012-10-13-2054.05.pdiff [4219B]

Get:6 http://apt.modmyi.com stable/main 2012-10-13-2054.05.pdiff [4219B]

Fetched 59.1kB in 9s (6221B/s)

Featured

11.9 aTV Flash enables you to install apps and packages on your Apple TV to add extra features.

● **Playing other media formats, including DVDs.** aTV Flash includes XBMC Media Center, which offers information and entertainment ranging from weather forecasts and Internet radio, to music and video playback from your network attached storage (NAS) device. XBMC can even play DVD files that you've copied from physical discs.

● **Surfing the Web.** The Browser app enables you to browse the Web without leaving your Apple TV. Typing URLs on the on-screen keyboard, shown in Figure 11.10, is cumbersome, but you can easily follow links and bookmark pages to return to later.

11.10 Use the Browser app to browse the Web on your Apple TV.

● **Keeping up with blogs and websites.** You can read RSS feeds directly on your Apple TV, as shown in Figure 11.11, which is great for staying up to date with your favorite sources of information.

● **Last.fm.** This service provides Internet radio that you can customize with your personal stations, as shown in Figure 11.12.

TUAW - The Unofficial Apple Weblog

Caturday: Cool breeze >

You're the Pundit: What will we get with the mini? >

Where are the extended battery cases for the iPhone 5? >

T8 Storm wallet case for iPhone 4/4S: Slim, light, and attractive >

One private Australian school now requiring iPads >

Wizkids and Marvel's HeroClix TabApp spoils its chance to innovate >

Apple to open third Beijing Apple Store on iconic Wangfujing Street >

iControlPad 2 reaches Kickstarter goal, shipping later this year >

Thieves smash car into Leawood, Kansas Apple Store >

11.11 aTV Flash includes an RSS reader for catching up on your reading.

Florence + the Machine Radio

Starry Eyed
Ellie Goulding
Lights

0:07 ▬▬◆━━━━━━━━━━━━━━━━━━ -2:49

"Starry Eyed" was the second single from Ellie Goulding's debut album Lights. It was released on 22nd February 2010 and reached number 4 in the UK Singles Charts. The song is the second track on the album Lights. Goulding explained the meaning of the song to Digital Spy: "It's about letting go. As opposed to all the sad and depressing things I write about, I decided to write something about the joining together of people in some kind of euphoric state - be it at a festival, at a show or in a club.

Powered by last.fm

11.12 Last.fm offers personalized radio listening.

How Can I Troubleshoot My Apple TV?

Reset

Choose Reset All Settings to reset your settings, including accounts and configuration.

Choose Restore to restore your Apple TV to its factory settings. Your Apple TV will also download and install the latest software update.

Cancel

Reset All Settings

Restore

Apple has made your Apple TV as elegant and straightforward as possible — but as with all hardware and software, problems may occur. In this chapter, I cover how to troubleshoot the problems you're most likely to experience. I start with how to keep your Apple TV updated, and then go through essential moves for recovering from hangs and crashes, as well as solving problems with remote controls, networking, displays, and Home Sharing. I also show you how to deal with content issues and problems with AirPlay, and how to use Apple Configurator to set up multiple Apple TVs.

Keeping Your Apple TV Updated **212**

Performing Essential Troubleshooting Moves **213**

Troubleshooting Remote Control Issues **218**

Troubleshooting Network and Internet Issues **220**

Troubleshooting Display Issues **230**

Troubleshooting Home Sharing Issues **232**

Troubleshooting Content Issues **239**

Troubleshooting AirPlay Issues **241**

Configuring an Apple TV Using Apple Configurator **252**

Keeping Your Apple TV Updated

To keep your Apple TV working well, you should keep your Apple TV's software updated. Updating also gives you any new features Apple adds and eliminates bugs that Apple has worked out of the system.

Here's how to update your Apple TV software:

1. **Press the Menu button one or more times until the Home screen appears.**

2. **Select Settings.** The Settings screen appears.

3. **Select General.** The General screen appears, as shown in Figure 12.1.

General

Name	Kitchen Apple TV ❯
Network	❯
Parental Controls	❯
Remotes	❯
Update Software	
Time Zone	San Francisco ❯
Sleep After	15 minutes
Send Data to Apple	No ❯
Language	❯

12.1 From the General screen, you can update your Apple TV software.

4. **Select Update Software.** Your Apple TV checks for a new version of its software. If there is one, the Apple TV downloads and installs it. Your Apple TV then restarts and you can use it as normal.

Interpreting the Apple TV Status Light

When all is well, you interact with your Apple TV using its sleek user interface. But when the Apple TV is having problems, its only means of communicating with you is by flashing its status light. Here's what the different alerts of the status light mean:

- **Status light is off.** The Apple TV is off.
- **Status light stays on.** The Apple TV is on.
- **Status light flashes once.** The Apple TV has accepted a remote command.
- **Status light flashes three times.** The Apple TV has rejected a remote command.
- **Status light flashes slowly.** The Apple TV is starting up.
- **Status light flashes rapidly.** The Apple TV is having problems.

Performing Essential Troubleshooting Moves

If your Apple TV starts behaving oddly, you may need to perform one or more of the following moves to get it working normally again:

- **Restart.** This action (also sometimes referred to as rebooting) powers down your Apple TV, and then powers it on again, reloading the operating system. Restarting can clear problems out of the device's memory, so it should be your first troubleshooting move.

- **Reset.** Resetting is a more serious move than restarting because it returns all of the Apple TV settings to their default values. This can help resolve problems, but it also means that you have to change the settings back to how you prefer them.

- **Restore.** This action is the most serious troubleshooting move. After you give the restore command, your Apple TV downloads the latest version of its operating system from the Apple servers, and then installs it. After the restore finishes, you need to set up your Apple TV again.

Restarting your Apple TV

You can restart your Apple TV from the user interface by using the Apple Remote or from the Apple TV itself. The following list explains how to perform these moves:

● **Restarting from the user interface.** If your Apple TV is still responding more or less normally to the remote control, you can follow these steps to restart it from the user interface:

   1. **Press the Menu button one or more times until the Home screen appears.**

   2. **Select Settings.** The Settings screen appears.

   3. **Select General.** The General screen appears.

   4. **Scroll all the way to the bottom, and then select Restart.**

● **Restarting using the Apple Remote.** If your Apple TV's user interface is frozen or not responding consistently, you can restart your Apple TV by using the Apple Remote. To restart, press the Menu and Down buttons simultaneously. Continue pressing them until the Apple TV status light starts to flash slowly to indicate that it's starting up, and then release the buttons.

● **Restarting without a remote.** If your Apple TV isn't responding to the remote, you can restart it the hard way: unplug the power cable, wait 30 seconds, and then plug it back in. After you plug in the cable, the Apple TV restarts automatically.

Resetting your Apple TV

If restarting your Apple TV doesn't make it work properly again, you can take your troubleshooting to the next stage, and reset the device. Resetting your Apple TV wipes out all of its custom settings and restores the default values. After you reset the Apple TV, you can change its settings back to how you like them.

Here's how to reset your Apple TV:

   1. **Press the Menu button one or more times until the Home screen appears.**

   2. **Select Settings.** The Settings screen appears.

   3. **Select General.** The General screen appears.

   4. **Scroll down almost to the bottom of the list, and then select Reset.** The Reset screen appears.

5. **Select Reset All Settings, as shown in Figure 12.2.** Your Apple TV shuts down, and then restarts with all settings reset to the defaults.

Reset

Choose Reset All Settings to reset your settings, including accounts and configuration.

Choose Restore to restore your Apple TV to its factory settings. Your Apple TV will also download and install the latest software update.

Cancel

Reset All Settings

Restore

12.2 From the Reset screen, you can reset all of the settings on your Apple TV.

Restoring your Apple TV

If resetting doesn't solve your Apple TV woes, you may need to restore it. This involves downloading the latest version of the Apple TV software and installing it with the default settings. After restoring, you have to set up your Apple TV again from scratch.

Note Restoring your Apple TV can take anywhere from a few minutes to an hour or so, depending on the speed of your Internet connection.

You can restore the Apple TV in either of the following ways:

- **Restore via the user interface.** Follow these steps to restore your Apple TV in the standard way:

  1. **Press the Menu button one or more times until the Home screen appears.**

  2. **Select Settings.** The Settings screen appears.

  3. **Select General.** The General screen appears.

4. **Scroll down almost to the bottom of the list, and then select Reset.** The Reset screen appears (see Figure 12.2).

5. **Select Restore.** The Apple TV downloads the latest software, installs it, and then restarts.

● **Restore using a micro USB cable.** If you're not able to restore your Apple TV as described above, you can also do so with a micro USB cable and your computer. The Apple TV doesn't include a micro USB cable, but it is the standard cable used by many electronic devices, such as phones and tablets. Before purchasing one, it's worth looking through your cable drawer to see if you already have one. Follow these steps to restore your Apple TV using a micro USB cable:

1. **Disconnect the power cable from the Apple TV.**

2. **Disconnect the HDMI cable from the Apple TV.**

3. **Connect the micro USB connector on the cable to the micro USB port on the back of the Apple TV.**

Caution

USB connectors come in both the micro (which is what you want here) and mini (which is confusingly similar but a little bigger) forms. If you have a USB cable with a small connector of indeterminate type, make sure that the connector matches the port on the back of the Apple TV before trying to insert it.

4. **Connect the standard USB connector on the cable to a USB port on your computer.**

5. **Connect the power cable to the Apple TV again.** The status light on the Apple TV starts flashing slowly, indicating that the device is starting up.

Genius

If you have a second-generation Apple TV, don't connect the power cable to the device. The USB cable provides enough power for the Apple TV.

6. **Open iTunes on your computer.** Your Apple TV appears in the Source list.

7. **Click your Apple TV in the Source list.** The control screen for the Apple TV appears, as shown in Figure 12.3.

12.3 Click your Apple TV in the Source list in iTunes to display the control screen.

8. **Click Restore.** iTunes displays the confirmation dialog shown in Figure 12.4.

9. **Click Restore and Update.** iTunes downloads and installs the latest version of the Apple TV software.

12.4 iTunes displays this confirmation dialog to make sure that you want to proceed with the restore.

Note

The confirmation dialog for restoring your Apple TV states that all of your media and other data will be erased. However, the Apple TV doesn't store your media — it streams media from other sources. This dialog is shared with iPhones, iPads, and iPods, which *do* store your media and data.

Troubleshooting Remote Control Issues

Because the Apple TV has no controls apart from its inputs, your only way to control it is by using a remote control. So it's important you know how to deal with any remote-control issues that arise.

Note You can use a different remote control than the Apple Remote if you like. See Chapter 9 for instructions on making your Apple TV recognize another remote control.

The Apple Remote controls your Mac instead of your Apple TV

If you find your Apple Remote is controlling your Mac instead of your Apple TV, you have the following two choices for fixing the problem:

- Pair the Apple Remote with your Apple TV so that the Apple Remote doesn't affect your Mac or other devices.

- Disable the remote-control receiver on your Mac.

Genius If you have a remote for your Mac, you can pair it with your Mac to prevent it from responding to other remotes. From the Advanced dialog in the Security & Privacy preferences, click the Pair button to start the pairing process, and then follow the instructions that appear.

Follow these steps to pair the Apple Remote with your Apple TV:

1. **Select Settings to display the Settings screen.**

2. **Select General to display the General screen.**

3. **Select Remotes to display the Remotes screen.**

4. **Select Pair Apple Remote.** The Apple TV pairs the remote, and the Unpair Apple Remote command appears in place of the Pair Apple Remote command.

Follow these steps to disable the remote-control receiver on your Mac:

1. **Choose Apple ⇨ System Preferences.** The System Preferences window opens.

2. **In the Personal section, click Security & Privacy.** The Security & Privacy pane appears.

3. **Click the General tab.** The General pane appears.

4. **Click the lock icon in the lower-left corner, type your password in the authentication dialog, and then click Unlock.** System Preferences unlocks the locked preferences.

5. **Click Advanced.** The Advanced dialog appears.

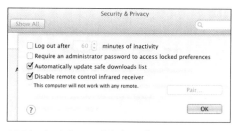

6. **Select the Disable remote control infrared receiver check box, as shown in Figure 12.5.**

12.5 In the Advanced dialog of Security & Privacy preferences, you can prevent your Mac from responding to your Apple Remote.

Your Apple TV doesn't respond to the Apple Remote

If your Apple TV doesn't respond to the Apple Remote, most likely the Apple TV has become paired with a different remote. To get the remote working again, you'll need to unpair the other remote from the Apple TV.

Genius

If your Apple TV is responding correctly to a remote, the status light flashes once each time that the Apple TV accepts a command you give by pressing a button on the remote. If the status light flashes three times, it means that the Apple TV has rejected the command.

Another possibility is that the Apple Remote has become paired with a different device. Normally, you'll notice quickly if this is the case, because pressing the buttons on the other remote will give commands. For example, if your Mac starts playing music in iTunes when you press Play/Pause on your Apple Remote, this means that the Apple Remote is commanding the Mac instead of the Apple TV. If the Apple Remote has become paired with another device, unpair it from that device.

Checking the Apple Remote battery

If your Apple TV stops responding to the Apple Remote, it's worth checking to see if the battery has run out of power. The battery lasts for weeks or months, depending on how much you use the remote, and then expires gracefully without putting up any warning flags.

To check whether the battery is working, open an app that displays your computer's webcam input, such as the following:

- **Mac.** Open Messages and choose Video ⇨ Preview to open a preview window. You can also launch iMovie and choose File ⇨ Import from Camera to open the Import window.

- **PC.** Launch Paint, click the Backstage tab (the unnamed tab to the left of the Home tab), and then choose From Scanner or Camera. If Windows prompts you to choose the scanner or camera, select the webcam.

After you've performed one of the actions above, aim the Apple Remote at the webcam and press any button. If you see a white flash from the top of the Apple Remote, it's working.

Note The cameras on the iPhone, iPod touch, and iPad can't pick up the signal from the Apple Remote, so you can't use these devices to check whether the remote's battery is working.

Troubleshooting Network and Internet Issues

Because your Apple TV contains no permanent storage, it needs a network or Internet connection to play back any content. Normally, you connect the Apple TV to your wired network or wireless network, which enables the device to use your Internet connection.

In this section, I show you how to troubleshoot wired network connection problems, wireless network connection problems, and Internet connection problems. You may also need to configure the Apple TV network settings manually, so I begin with a quick reminder about that.

Manually configuring the Apple TV network settings

If your network uses Dynamic Host Configuration Protocol (DHCP) to provide computers and devices with network configuration information, your Apple TV automatically gets its Internet Protocol (IP) address and other configuration information. Most home networks use DHCP, because it is built into most broadband routers and is easy and convenient to use.

If your network doesn't use DHCP, you have to configure the Apple TV network settings manually. You can do this for either a wired network or a wireless network. You need four pieces of information: The subnet mask, and the IP, router, and DNS server addresses (see the sidebar about TCP/IP addressing for more information).

Understanding TCP/IP Addressing

Transmission Control Protocol/Internet Protocol (TCP/IP) comes in two main versions: Internet Protocol version 4 (IPv4), which I cover here, and Internet Protocol version 6 (IPv6). IPv4 is the version most widely used in North America and Europe. IPv6 is newer and better, but the transition from IPv4 to IPv6 is proving a slow, awkward, and expensive process.

TCP/IP uses the following pieces of information to configure a computer or device:

- **IP address.** This is a four-part number in dotted-decimal notation, such as 192.168.0.100 or 10.0.0.255. Each part is a number in the range of 0 to 256. Most home networks use the 192.168.0.x or 192.168.1.x address range.

- **Subnet mask.** A network can be broken into a number of subdivisions called subnets. The subnet mask is a four-part number that tells the computer which subnet to use. Almost all home networks use the subnet mask 255.255.255.0.

- **Router address.** This is the IP address of the router that's directing traffic around the network. In a home network, the router address is usually a low-numbered address in the subnet — for example, 192.168.0.1 or 192.168.1.1.

- **DNS server address.** This is the IP address of the Domain Name System (DNS) server that tells the computer how to resolve web addresses (such as www.google.com) to IP addresses (such as 173.194.41.70).

Follow these steps to manually configure the Apple TV network settings:

1. **From the Home screen, select Settings.** The Setting screen appears.

2. **Select General.** The General screen appears.

3. **Select Network.** The Network screen appears, as shown in Figure 12.6.

Network

Configure Wi-Fi   >

Configure TCP/IP   >

Test Network   >

Network Name	HD
IP Address	DHCP 10.0.0.43
Subnet Mask	255.255.255.0
Router Address	10.0.0.2
DNS Address	10.0.0.2
Wi-Fi Address	58:55:ca:0d:36:57
Signal Strength	▪▪▪▪▪

To switch to Ethernet, connect an Ethernet cable to your Apple TV.

12.6 On the Network screen, you can start manually configuring the Apple TV network connection.

4. **Select Configure TCP/IP.** The Network Setup screen appears.

5. **Select Manually, as shown in Figure 12.7, to display the first Ethernet TCP/IP Setup screen, on which you can set the IP address.**

Network Setup

For most networks, automatic configuration is sufficient. If you have a custom network with specifically assigned IP addresses, choose Manually.

Configure IP: Automatically

Manually

12.7 On the Network Setup screen, select Manually.

6. **Set the IP address that you want the Apple TV to use, as shown in Figure 12.8.** Press the Right and Left buttons to navigate to the figure that you want to change. Press the Up button to increase the number, or the Down button to decrease it.

Ethernet TCP/IP Setup

Enter the IP address for your Apple TV and then select Done.

IP Address: 0 1 0 . 0 0 0 . 0 0 0 . 0 3 7 **DONE**

12.8 On the Ethernet TCP/IP Setup screen, use the remote to set the IP address.

7. **Select Done.** Your Apple TV displays the second Ethernet TCP/IP Setup screen, on which you can set the subnet mask.

8. **Follow through the remaining screens to set the router and DNS server addresses.**

Fixing incorrect network settings

If your Apple TV loses its network connection, you notice pretty fast because the network-dependent items disappear from the Home screen. For example, when the icons for Movies, TV Shows, and Music vanish, the Apple TV has lost its network connection. First, check that your router is working. If it isn't, restart it.

If the router is running fine, and other computers and devices can connect to the Internet through the router, try restarting the Apple TV. If your network doesn't use DHCP, check through the settings on your Apple TV as described in the previous section. Any of the following problems can cause the Apple TV to lose its network connection:

- **IP address conflict.** If you've manually set the Apple TV's IP address but use DHCP for other computers and devices on the network, the DHCP server may have assigned the Apple TV's IP address to another computer or device while the Apple TV was off or asleep. If this has happened, you need to change the IP address on either the Apple TV or the other computer or device. One way you can do this is by restarting the other computer or device while the Apple TV is awake. This causes the computer or device to request another IP address.

Genius

You can avoid IP address conflicts by setting the DHCP server in your router to use a pool of IP addresses that do not overlap those you assign manually.

- **The subnet mask is wrong.** Using the wrong subnet mask puts the Apple TV on the wrong part of the network. For most home networks, you need the 255.255.255.0 subnet mask.

- **The router address is wrong.** Setting the wrong IP address for the router knocks the Apple TV off the network.

- **The DNS server address is wrong.** Setting the wrong IP address for the DNS server allows the Apple TV to reach computers on your local network but prevents it from finding Internet addresses. For example, if you get a message that says *The iTunes Store is currently unavailable. Try again later*, you should check the DNS server address that the Apple TV is using.

Troubleshooting wired network connection issues

After you connect your Apple TV to your wired network, the network connection should simply work unless the cables are disconnected or severed. So if your Apple TV loses its connection to the wired network, destructive creatures such as mice, dogs, or children may have been at work.

First, check that the rest of the wired network is okay. Check your broadband router or network router to see if its error light is blinking; if so, restart it. If the router is okay, see if another computer connected to the network can still access the network and the Internet. If it can, the problem is confined to your Apple TV.

Next, make sure the cable or cables to the Apple TV have sustained no physical damage and are securely connected at both ends. If the cables seem okay, but the problem persists, try swapping each suspect cable in turn for a known good cable to see if there's a hidden problem.

Troubleshooting wireless network connection issues

Today's wireless networks are far more advanced than their predecessors. However, they still tend to have more problems than wired networks. This section shows you how to resolve the wireless network problems you're most likely to encounter with your Apple TV.

Genius

For video streaming, the Apple TV needs a wireless network that uses 801.11a, 802.11g, or 802.11n, and not 802.11b. This is because an 802.11b connection has a maximum data rate of 11Mbps, which is too slow for streaming video consistently. If you're looking to get a new wireless router, go for 802.11n.

The Apple TV loses its wireless connection

If your Apple TV periodically loses its connection to the wireless network, it may be positioned at or near the limit of the wireless router's range. To see the strength of the signal that the Apple TV is getting, choose Settings ➪ General ➪ About, and look at the Signal Strength readout at the bottom of the About screen (shown in Figure 12.9) or the Network screen. The range goes from one bar (a weak signal) to five bars (a strong signal).

	About	
Name		Living Room Apple TV
Model		MC572FD/A
Serial Number		DCYDM7WBDDR5
Apple TV Software		5.0.2 (4250)
TV Resolution		720p HD - 60Hz
Wi-Fi Network		HD
IP Address		DHCP 10.0.0.43
Wi-Fi Address		58:55:ca:0d:36:57
Signal Strength		▪▪▪▪▪

12.9 You can check the signal strength of the wireless connection on the About screen.

If you see only a bar or two, consider moving the Apple TV nearer to the wireless router (or moving the router nearer to the Apple TV, if that's easier) or adding an antenna or a booster to the router to strengthen the signal.

Note The Signal Strength readout tells you the strength of the wireless signal that your Apple TV is getting, but not how much interference it's suffering. If there's a lot of interference, the data rate may be low. This is like the trouble you might have picking out words at a loud party, even when someone is shouting in your ear. Conversely, if your home is silent, you can hear a whisper — a weak signal — from a good distance away.

The Apple TV has a wireless connection but no Internet connection

If the Apple TV has a wireless connection but no Internet connection, check that it's connected to the right network. Normally, this is a problem only if you've connected your Apple TV to two or more wireless networks in the past — but these days, many people have multiple wireless networks in their dwellings, so connecting the Apple TV to more than one network isn't that unusual. To see which wireless network your Apple TV is connected to, choose Settings ⇨ General ⇨ Network, and then look at the Network Name readout, as shown in Figure 12.10.

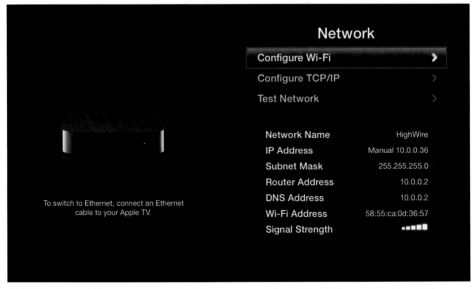

12.10 The Network Name readout on the Network screen shows the wireless network to which your Apple TV has connected.

Note

You can also see the network's name on the About screen, but the Network screen is a better place to start fixing a problem.

If the Apple TV is connected to the wrong wireless network, choose Configure Wi-Fi to display the Wi-Fi Network screen. Next, select the wireless network, as shown in Figure 12.11, and then enter the password if the Apple TV prompts you to do so. If the wireless network is *closed* — meaning that it doesn't broadcast its network name — select Other on the Wi-Fi Network screen. On the resulting screen, type the network name, and then select Submit.

🛜 **Wi-Fi Network**

To connect to the Internet, choose your Wi-Fi network, or connect using an ethernet cable. If you don't see your Wi-Fi network, select Other.

AirPort Express

HD

HighWire

Surreal Macs AP

Surreal Macs AP01

Surreal Macs AP02

Surreal Macs AP03

Other...

12.11 On the Wi-Fi Network screen, choose the network to which you want to connect your Apple TV.

Genius

If you have just restarted your wireless router, you may find that the wireless network doesn't appear on the Wi-Fi Network screen. This screen doesn't automatically update, so don't wait for the network to appear. Instead, press the Menu button to go back to the Network screen, and then select Configure Wi-Fi again. This makes your Apple TV scan again for wireless networks.

The Apple TV claims the Wi-Fi password is incorrect

If you enter the password for a wireless network correctly, but the Apple TV gives the message *The Wi-Fi password you entered is not correct*, check whether the wireless network uses WPA Enterprise or WPA2 Enterprise encryption.

The Apple TV can't connect to networks that use WPA Enterprise or WPA2 Enterprise, so if the wireless network is yours, change the encryption to WPA2. This provides plenty of protection unless you're actively in trouble with the security services.

Troubleshooting Internet connection issues

Because it streams its content, your Apple TV relies heavily on your Internet connection. This section shows you what to do if your Apple TV loses its Internet connection or if the Apple TV claims the iTunes Store is currently unavailable.

Your Apple TV loses its Internet connection

If your Apple TV suddenly loses its Internet connection, first check whether your other computers still have working connections to the Internet. If so, the problem lies with your connection. If not, restart your Internet router and see if it can reestablish the connection.

Caution   Unlike most other computers and devices, the Apple TV gives no error message when it suffers an IP address conflict — that is, when the Apple TV is trying to use the same IP address as another device on the network. When an IP address conflict occurs, the Apple TV simply loses its Internet connection.

If your Apple TV is the only device without a working Internet connection, the problem likely lies with the Apple TV itself. Here's how to solve this problem:

1. **Check the physical connection:**

    *   **Wired connection.** Check that the cable is intact and plugged firmly into both the Apple TV, and the network switch or router.

    *   **Wireless connection.** Check that the wireless router is working. The easiest way to do so is by using another computer or device that connects to the wireless network. If the computer or device connects to the Internet, the connection is working; if not, restart the wireless router.

2. **Perform the following actions to check the Apple TV network setup:**

    *   **From the Home screen, select Settings ➪ General ➪ Network.** The Network screen appears.

    *   **Check whether the Apple TV is using a wired or wireless connection.** If the Configure Wi-Fi item appears on the Network screen (see Figure 12.10), the Apple TV is using a wireless connection. Otherwise, it's using a wired connection.

    *   **Select Configure TCP/IP.** The Network Setup screen appears.

    *   **If your network uses DHCP, select Automatically.** Otherwise, select Manually, and then follow the prompts to set the subnet mask, and the IP, router, and DNS server addresses.

3. **Restart the Apple TV if necessary.**

Genius

Usually, it's easy enough to check whether your Apple TV has a working Internet connection. If apps, such as Movies, can display content, your Internet connection is okay. If you're not sure whether the Internet connection is working, choose Settings ➪ General ➪ Network ➪ Test Network. The Network Test feature mostly provides information to Apple rather than to you, but it will certainly let you know if your Internet connection isn't working.

You get a message that the iTunes Store is unavailable

If your Apple TV's Home screen shows the full complement of apps, but you get the message *The iTunes Store is currently unavailable. Try again later*, the Apple TV is suffering from a DNS problem. If you've set your network configuration manually, you may have entered the wrong address for the DNS server. Select Settings ➪ General ➪ Network from the Home screen to display the Network screen, and then look at the DNS Address readout.

If the address is wrong, select Configure TCP/IP, select Manually, and then go through the configuration screens until you reach the TCP/IP Setup screen or Wi-Fi TCP/IP Setup screen for setting the DNS address shown in Figure 12.12. Correct the IP address, and then select Done. If your Apple TV has the right IP address for the DNS server, but the Apple TV can't reach the iTunes Store, check that your Internet connection is working for your other computers and devices. If your ISP's DNS server has gone down for the count, none of your computers and devices will be able to access websites until the server is working again.

12.12 Correcting the DNS address can solve problems accessing the iTunes Store.

Troubleshooting Display Issues

In this section, I cover how to troubleshoot various display issues, including videos not appearing, playback disruptions, and content icons not appearing on the Home screen.

No video appears on the TV screen

If no video appears on the TV screen, the problem may lie with the Apple TV, the connection cable or connection equipment, or the output resolution. Here's how to troubleshoot this problem:

1. **First, verify that the Apple TV is powered on in one of the following ways:**

    - **If the status light is glowing, you're in business.**

    - **If the status light is not on, make sure that the Apple TV power cable is connected to both the device and the electrical socket.**

    - **If the power cable is firmly connected, but no status light appears, make sure the electrical socket is working.** For example, plug in a lamp and switch it on to verify that there's power.

2. **Check the following connections between the Apple TV and the TV:**

    - **Make sure that each cable is firmly plugged in.**

    - **If you're using an HDMI hub to make the connection, remove it, and then make the connection directly.**

Note   The standard way of connecting the Apple TV to a TV is an HDMI cable. If your TV lacks an HDMI input, you need an HDMI-to–Component Video converter or an HDMI-to–Component Video converter, plus the appropriate cables. See Chapter 1 for details on these connection options.

    - **Make sure each cable is intact — for example, that it hasn't been chewed or severed.**

    - **If you're using a converter box that requires power, verify that its power supply is working.** For example, check that the status light on the converter box is lit.

3. **Check that the TV has the correct input selected.** How you do this depends on the TV model (see the manual that came with it), but it's usually straightforward.

4. **Perform the following actions to cycle through the resolutions on the Apple TV:**

   - **To start cycling, press the Menu and Up buttons simultaneously for about six seconds.** The Apple TV displays the next resolution for about 20 seconds, and then switches to the next one.

   - **To move straight to the next resolution, press the Select button.**

   - **To accept the current resolution, press the Menu button.**

Video playback is choppy or interrupted

If you find that video playback is choppy or interrupted, your first suspect should be your Internet connection. That's because this problem normally indicates the Apple TV isn't getting a fast enough data stream to display the video smoothly. First, look at your Internet router's status screen to see how fast your connection speed currently is. This will tell you if the Apple TV should be able to get a steady stream. See the sidebar about choosing resolution for more information about the speeds you typically need for streaming.

Genius   To get a real-world reading of your Internet connection's throughput, open a web browser on a computer on your network, and navigate to a speed-test site, such as Speedtest.net (www.speedtest.net).

If your Internet connection speed seems high but your Apple TV still can't play back video satisfactorily, check what the other computers and devices on the network are doing. If one of your housemates is running a file-sharing server or downloading the Library of Congress, less of the Internet connection's capacity will be available for streaming video. If the problem seems to be confined to your Apple TV, restart it.

App icons disappear from the Home screen

If the icons for any apps disappear from the Home screen, your Apple TV has lost its Internet connection. See the section on troubleshooting network and Internet issues earlier in this chapter for ways to fix this problem.

Choosing a Suitable Video Resolution for Your Internet Connection

The Apple TV version 3 can play video in full 1080p resolution, which provides the best viewing quality but also requires the largest amount of data to be transferred. If you find your Internet connection can't deliver the data fast enough, you can reduce the resolution to 720p or Standard Definition to lower the bandwidth needed.

The following are the minimum bandwidths in megabits per second (Mbps) that Apple recommends for trouble-free video streaming:

- 1080p, 8 Mbps
- 720p, 6 Mbps
- Standard Definition, 2.5 Mbps

These are sustained speeds rather than peak speeds. So if your Internet connection's speed goes up and down depending on what your neighbors are doing, you may be able to stream 1080p video satisfactorily at some times but not at others.

Here's how to reduce the resolution:

1. **From the Home screen, select Settings.** The Settings screen appears.
2. **Select iTunes Store.** The iTunes Store screen appears.
3. **Highlight Video Resolution, and then press the Select button one or more times to cycle through the available resolutions.**

If you have an Apple TV version 2, your top resolution is 720p, so you may not experience choppy video. If you do, reduce the resolution to Standard Definition.

Troubleshooting Home Sharing Issues

As you saw in Chapter 4, Apple's Home Sharing technology gives you great freedom and flexibility by sharing music, videos, and other files among your computers, iOS devices, and Apple TVs. This section covers how to provide the conditions that Home Sharing needs to work correctly. It also explains how to deal with authorization problems and connection problems that can occur with Home Sharing.

Providing the conditions Home Sharing needs

If Home Sharing isn't working, make sure that you're giving it the conditions it needs. This means updating your computers to the latest version of iTunes, your iOS devices to the latest version of iOS, and your Apple TV to the latest version of its firmware; making sure your Internet connection is working properly; checking for other network issues; and using the same Apple ID on each computer and device.

Note To enable Home Sharing to perform optimally, update your Apple TV to the latest version of its software. Follow the instructions for doing so covered earlier in this chapter.

Updating to the latest version of iTunes

For best results, make sure your computer is running the latest version of iTunes. To do so, open iTunes and choose iTunes ⌴ Check for Updates. If your computer displays a dialog saying that this version of iTunes is the current version, click OK. Otherwise, follow the prompts to download and install the newest version of iTunes.

Note On a Mac, you can also choose Apple ⌴ Software Update to check for all available updates, including updates to iTunes.

Updating your iOS devices

You can update your iOS devices to the latest version of the iOS software in either of the following ways:

- **Update using a computer by following these steps:**
    1. **Connect the iOS device to the computer via the USB cable.**
    2. **Open iTunes if your computer doesn't open it automatically.**
    3. **Click the iOS device in the Source list on the left of the iTunes window.** The control screens for the device appear.
    4. **If the Summary screen isn't displayed, click the Summary tab to display it.**
    5. **Click Check for Update.** If iTunes finds an update, follow the prompts to download and install it.

- **Update on the iOS device.** From the Home screen, choose
  Settings ⇨ General ⇨ Software Update. If Software Update finds an update, follow the
  prompts to download and install it.

Checking your Internet connection

These days, an Internet connection is so vital to life and leisure that you probably notice its absence within moments if it goes down. Even if you're not using the Internet when the service breaks down, chances are another member of your household is and will raise the alarm.

Note

Home Sharing requires an Internet connection in order to work because Home Sharing uses your Apple ID to ensure that each computer or device that requests access to a shared library is authorized to access it.

The easiest way to make sure your Internet connection is working is to open your default browser and see if your home page loads. For example, on a Mac, click the Safari icon on the Dock; in Windows, click the Internet Explorer icon. If your Internet connection isn't working, restore it as normal. For example, restart your Internet router.

Checking for other network issues

If your Internet connection is working but Home Sharing isn't, check for the following network issues:

- On a wired network, look for physical problems, such as disconnected or damaged cables, as discussed earlier in this chapter.
- On a wireless network, restart the wireless router if necessary.
- Make sure that other computers can access the Internet through the network.
- If you have chosen network settings manually, verify that they are correct.

Note

For Home Sharing, all of the computers and devices must be on the same network. In technical terms, they must be on the same TCP/IP *subnet*, which is a logical division of a physical network. Normally, this is the case for a home network. However, if you have used a router to create different subnets (something you might do to protect your work computers from your kids' computers), Home Sharing doesn't work from one subnet to another.

Using the same Apple ID on each computer and device

Home Sharing works only if each computer or device uses the same Apple ID. If you have only a single Apple ID, this won't be a problem. However, if you're among the increasing number of people who find that they need multiple Apple IDs, make sure that your computers and devices are using the same one.

Here's how to check which Apple ID your computers and devices are using:

- **Mac or PC.** Open the Advanced menu and look at the Turn Off Home Sharing command. The Apple ID appears in parentheses after the command, as shown in Figure 12.13.

- **iPhone, iPod touch, or iPad.** From the Home screen, tap Settings, tap Music, and then look at the Home Sharing area.

- **Apple TV.** From the Home screen, choose Settings ⇨ Computers, and then look at the lower-left corner of the screen.

12.13 The Turn Off Home Sharing command shows the Apple ID that iTunes is using for sharing.

Troubleshooting authorization problems

Home Sharing uses what Apple calls *authorization* to control which computers can play which music. At this writing, you can authorize up to five computers at a time. Once you hit that limit, you need to deauthorize one or more of them before you can use Home Sharing with another computer.

The following list explains how to deauthorize a single computer or all of your computers:

- **Deauthorize a single computer.** If you still have the computer and it's still running, open iTunes, choose Store ⇨ Deauthorize This Computer. Enter your Apple ID and password, as shown in Figure 12.14, and then click Deauthorize.

12.14 Use the Deauthorize This Computer dialog to deauthorize a single computer.

● **Deauthorize all of your computers.** If you no longer have the computer that you need to deauthorize (or if you do but it's not working), you can deauthorize all of your computers, and then reauthorize the others. To deauthorize all of your computers, follow these steps:

1. **Open iTunes.**

2. **Choose Store ⇨ View My Account.**

3. **If the Enter Password dialog appears, type your password, and then click View Account.** The Account Information screen appears.

4. **In the Apple ID Summary box, click Deauthorize All, and then follow the prompts.**

Genius

If your household has more than five computers, you may find Home Sharing's five-computer limit restrictive. The only workarounds are either to use regular sharing (which you set up on the Sharing tab in iTunes preferences) instead of Home Sharing for some computers, or to set up another Apple ID and create a separate Home Sharing group. The latter approach can work well if you're sharing different types of music, such as one for parents and another for kids.

Troubleshooting connection issues

If you're unable to connect successfully to your shared iTunes libraries, try as many of the steps explained in the following sections as necessary to restore the connection. Stop when Home Sharing is working again.

Before troubleshooting your connection to shared iTunes libraries, make sure that your Internet connection is working. The easiest way to do this is to try connecting to the Internet using one of your computers or devices. If a web browser can display a web page, the connection is okay. If the Internet connection isn't working, you may need to restart your Internet router.

Restarting iTunes

If you're unable to access a particular shared library, try restarting iTunes on that computer in one of the following ways:

● **Mac.** Activate iTunes, and then press ⌘+Q. Click the iTunes icon on the Dock.

● **PC.** Activate iTunes, and then press Alt+F4. Open the Start menu, and then click iTunes.

Restarting your computer

If restarting iTunes doesn't solve the problem, try restarting the Mac or PC that you can't reach:

- **Mac.** Click Apple to display the Apple menu, hold down Option, and then click Restart.

- **PC.** Click the Start button, click the right-arrow button to the right of the Shut Down button on the Start menu, and then click Restart.

Restarting Home Sharing

If restarting your computer doesn't solve the problem, try turning Home Sharing off and on again like this:

1. **Launch or activate iTunes.**

2. **Choose Advanced ⇨ Turn Off Home Sharing.** iTunes turns off Home Sharing without confirmation or comment.

3. **Choose Advanced ⇨ Turn On Home Sharing.** iTunes displays the Home Sharing screen.

4. **Type your Apple ID if necessary.**

5. **Type your password.**

6. **Click Create Home Share.** iTunes turns on Home Sharing and displays a message saying that it is on.

7. **Click Done.**

Turning on the wake for network access feature on a Mac

If the shared library that you're trying to access is on a Mac, make sure that the wake for network access feature is turned on. Otherwise, Home Sharing won't be able to rouse the Mac if it's asleep.

Here's how to turn on the wake for network access feature:

1. **Choose Apple ⇨ System Preferences.**

2. **Choose View ⇨ Energy Saver.** Alternatively, click the Energy Saver icon in the Hardware section.

Setting a PC to Wake for Network Access

You can set some PCs to wake for network access, although it usually only works for wired connections. The specifics vary depending on the model, but these are the general steps:

1. **Enable Wake-on-LAN in your computer's Basic Input/Output System (BIOS).** To access the BIOS, restart your computer, look for the onscreen prompt telling you which key to press, and then press it.

2. **Open Device Manager from the Control Panel in Windows.** In the Network Adapters category, right-click the Ethernet card, and then click Properties. When it opens, click the Advanced tab. In the Property list, select the appropriate check box (look for Wake on LAN or Wake on Magic Packet). Click OK.

3. **In the Control Panel, click Programs and Features, and then click Turn Windows Features On or Off in the left panel.** Select the Simple TCP/IP Services check box, and then click OK.

4. **Again in the Control Panel, click Administrative Tools, and then double-click Services.** In the Services window, double-click Simple TCP/IP Services. In the Properties dialog, choose Automatic in the Startup Type drop-down list, and then click Start if the service is not already running. Click OK.

5. **Click Windows Firewall with Advanced Security in the Administrative Tools window.** The window opens. Right-click Inbound Rules in the left pane, and then click New Rule. Follow the screens to open UDP port 9 and allow the Wake-on-LAN feature to cross the Windows Firewall.

Genius

If the System Preferences icon appears on the Dock, Control+click or right-click it, and then click Energy Saver on the pop-up menu.

3. Select the Wake for network access check box, as shown in Figure 12.15.

4. Click the Close button (the red button) at the left end of the title bar, or choose System Preferences ⇨ Quit System Preferences.

12.15 You can turn on the wake for network access feature in the Energy Saver pane on a Mac.

Troubleshooting Content Issues

In this section, I cover how to deal with content issues that you may experience with your Apple TV. These issues include the Movies and TV Shows apps not appearing on the Home screen; getting an error message that your Apple TV is not authorized to play a movie or show, even though you purchased it with the correct account; getting an HDCP (High-Bandwidth Digital Content Protection) error; or if you are unable to play content from the iTunes Store.

The Movies and TV Shows apps don't appear on the Home screen

If the Movies and TV Shows apps don't appear on the Apple TV's Home screen, you may have connected to the iTunes Store in the wrong country. Try changing the country like this:

1. **Press the Menu button one or more times to display the Home screen.**

2. **Select Settings.** The Settings screen appears.

3. **Select iTunes Store.** The iTunes Store screen appears.

4. **If the Location readout shows the wrong country, select Location, select the right country on the Location screen, and then press the Menu button.**

The Apple TV says it's not authorized to play content

If you see this message: *Your Apple TV is not authorized to play this content*, it normally indicates that you're trying to play DRM-protected content on an unauthorized device.

> **Note**
>
> DRM is the abbreviation for digital rights management, a type of technology for limiting the actions you can take with a digital file. DRM is typically applied to protect the interests of copyright holders. For example, when you buy a movie from the iTunes Store, DRM links the movie to your Apple ID, so that you can play the movie only on devices authorized with your Apple ID.

This message also sometimes appears when you try to use your Apple TV to play content you've purchased on another computer or device — such as in iTunes or on your iPhone — even though your Apple TV is authorized with your Apple ID.

When you run into this message, first verify that your Apple TV is indeed authorized with the same Apple ID. From the Home screen, select Settings ➪ iTunes Store, and then look at the Sign Out readout to make sure it shows the correct Apple ID. If not, select Sign Out, select Sign In, and then sign in with the correct Apple ID.

When the Apple ID is correct, there's not a single solution to this problem. Try the following four troubleshooting maneuvers in order until the problem stops:

- **Sign out of the iTunes Store, and then sign back in.** From the Home screen, select Settings ➪ iTunes Store, and then select Sign Out. Once signed out, select Sign In.

- **Restart your Apple TV.** From the Home screen, select Settings ➪ General ➪ Restart. Restarting forces the Apple TV to reread its settings, so it may clear up the problem.

- **Buy a free movie or show from the iTunes Store.** From the Home screen, select Movies or TV Shows (as appropriate). Navigate to a free item, select it, and then purchase it. Using your Apple ID on the Apple TV like this may sort out the settings.

- **Contact Apple Support.** If none of the previously listed moves clear up the problem, ask Apple for help.

Your Apple TV gives you an HDCP error

If your Apple TV gives you an HDCP (High-Bandwidth Digital Content Protection) error when you try to play high-quality video content, take a close look at the HDMI cable you're using to connect your Apple TV to your TV or monitor.

Understanding High-Bandwidth Digital Content Protection (HDCP)

High-Bandwidth Digital Content Protection (HDCP) is a security technology for protecting digital content against copyright infringement. Like many similar technologies, it's helpful to the copyright holders but not to consumers.

HDCP encrypts the digital output from the playback device and the display to prevent a "man-in-the-middle" attack from intercepting the content (and doing something nefarious with it). If you like to know technical terms, the playback device is the HDCP *source* and the display is the HDCP *sink*. You can also put an HDCP repeater between the source and the sink to get greater distance.

So, when you play back HDCP content, your Apple TV puts out an encrypted video stream, and the TV or monitor decrypts it. If the cable can't carry the encrypted signal cleanly, you get an error.

First, make sure the connections are made solidly on each end. If the error still occurs, you may need to replace the cable with an HDCP-certified cable. These cables cost only a few dollars each, so this is a relatively painless troubleshooting step. HDCP-certified products normally advertise the fact prominently as a selling point, but if you're not sure whether a product is certified, look at the Digital Content Protection website (www.digital-cp.com/hdcp_products).

The Apple TV can't play content from the iTunes Store

If your Apple TV can't play content from the iTunes Store, your router may be blocking the ports the iTunes Store requires. If your router is causing the problem, and your computers or iOS devices are connected to the same network, they'll have problems playing iTunes Store content as well.

To enable playback of iTunes Store content, go into your router's configuration screens and open TCP ports 80 and 443. How you do this depends on the router, but you'll normally find the relevant controls on the Firewall screen.

Troubleshooting AirPlay Issues

As you saw earlier in this book, AirPlay enables you to stream music or video from your computer or iOS device (iPhone, iPod touch, or iPad) to your Apple TV or another device that supports AirPlay. AirPlay is great for the Apple TV because you can easily share content from your iOS device or computer on a big screen. If you're lucky, AirPlay works seamlessly, but you may find that the AirPlay icon goes missing or that AirPlay playback stutters, skips, or drops out.

Genius

Many of the built-in apps on the iPhone, iPod touch, and iPad support AirPlay. But only some third-party apps support it. If you're trying to use AirPlay with a third-party app, check first that the app supports AirPlay before spending time troubleshooting its failure to do so.

The AirPlay icon is missing from iTunes or your iOS device

If the AirPlay icon doesn't appear in the lower-right corner of the iTunes window or the recently-used apps list on your iOS device, follow these steps to get it back:

1. **Perform the following actions to verify that AirPlay is enabled for the Apple TV:**

   ● **From the Home screen, choose Settings.** The Settings screen appears.

   ● **Choose AirPlay.** The AirPlay screen appears.

   ● **If the AirPlay readout says On, as shown in Figure 12.16, you're in business.** Otherwise, select AirPlay to change the status to On.

2. **Restart iTunes or your iOS device.** Restarting forces the app or the iOS device to reset its settings, so this can be an easy way to clear out problems.

AirPlay

| AirPlay | On |
| Set Password | > |

AirPlay lets you wirelessly view content on your TV from your iPhone, iPad, iPod touch, or iTunes on your computer.

Go to www.apple.com/support/appletv for more information.

12.16 Look at the AirPlay readout on the AirPlay screen to verify that AirPlay is on.

3. **Update your computers and devices to the latest versions of available software in the following ways:**

    - **Mac.** Choose Apple ⇨ Software Update.

    - **PC.** Choose Help ⇨ Check for Updates.

    - **iPhone, iPod touch, or iPad.** Choose Settings ⇨ General ⇨ Software Update.

    - **Apple TV.** Choose Settings ⇨ General ⇨ Update Software.

4. **Update your network router to the latest version of its firmware.** How you do this depends on the router, but you normally find an Update screen in the router's settings.

5. **If the device that has lost AirPlay is an iOS device, make sure that Wi-Fi is on.** Choose Settings and look at the Wi-Fi readout. If a network name appears, make sure that it's the right one. If Off appears, perform the following actions to connect to the network:

    - **Tap Wi-Fi.** The Wi-Fi screen appears, as shown in Figure 12.17.

    - **If it is turned off, tap the Wi-Fi switch and move it to the On position.**

    - **If your device doesn't automatically join the right network, tap the network in the Choose a Network list (see Figure 12.18).** Type the password if iOS prompts you for it.

12.17 Check the Wi-Fi screen to make sure that Wi-Fi is turned on.

12.18 Select the Wi-Fi network that you want to use.

6. **If you're using Wi-Fi, perform one of the following actions to ensure that the computer or device is connected to the same network as the Apple TV:**

- **Mac.** Click the Wi-Fi icon in the menu bar to see which name has a check mark next to it, as shown in Figure 12.19.

- **PC.** Click the Wireless Network icon in the notification area and look at the name in the Currently connected to box at the top of the menu, as shown in Figure 12.20. If you prefer, you can also hold the mouse pointer over the Wireless Network icon and look at the ScreenTip that appears.

- **iOS device.** From the Home screen, tap Settings, and then look at the name on the Wi-Fi button.

- **Apple TV.** From the Home screen, choose Settings ➪ General ➪ Network, and then look at the Network Name readout.

7. **Make sure the computer or device can connect to the Internet.** For example, launch Safari or another web browser on the computer or device. If it doesn't have an Internet connection, try restarting it.

12.19 In OS X, you can find the name of the wireless network by clicking the Wi-Fi icon on the menu bar.

12.20 On a PC, you can reveal the name of the wireless network by clicking the Wireless Network icon in the notification area.

8. **Set your network router to allow multicast streams.** How you do this depends on your router's make and model, so you may need to do some sleuthing, but here are some examples:

- **D-Link.** Choose Advanced ⇨ Advanced Network. Select the Enable Multicast Streams check box in the Multicast Streams area, and then click Save Settings.

Genius Some network routers block multicast streams because they can cause performance problems on the network. If your router blocks multicast streams, you have to turn off the blocking to get AirPlay to work.

- **Linksys.** Choose Router Admin ⇨ Security ⇨ Firewall, select the Enable Multicast check box, and then click Save.

- **NETGEAR.** In the Advanced section of the Navigation pane, click QoS Setup. On the QoS Setup screen that appears, deselect the Block Multicast/Broadcast MAC Address check box (MAC is the acronym for Media Access Control). Then click Apply.

Genius If you have a NETGEAR router, click the Wireless tab and make sure the Enable Wireless Isolation check box is deselected. The Wireless Isolation feature is for giving your wireless computers and devices an Internet connection only — it prevents them from connecting to the rest of the wireless network, so AirPlay won't work.

- **Other routers.** Search online for AirPlay, and your router's make and model. If you find nothing specific, try opening ports 443, 554, 3689, and 5353 on the router.

Note Some older routers don't support multicast, so you can't use AirPlay with them. If you're planning to buy a new router, download its specification sheet and make sure it does support multicast and AirPlay.

AirPlay playback is disrupted

If AirPlay works, but you find that the playback stutters, skips, or drops out altogether, try the fixes covered in this section.

Note

Ethernet cables can be up to 100 meters (327 feet) long, so unless you have a king-size residence, distance shouldn't be a problem. But drilling through floors and base-boards may be.

Connect your Apple TV via Ethernet

If possible, connect your Apple TV to a wired network rather than a wireless one. Normally, a wired network provides significantly better performance, even when you're using AirPlay from a device that must use the wireless network (such as an iPhone or iPad).

Turn off Bluetooth on your iOS device

If you're using an iPhone, iPod touch, or iPad for AirPlay, turn off Bluetooth while using AirPlay. Bluetooth is a great feature on iOS devices, but it can also interfere with AirPlay.

Here's how to turn off Bluetooth:

1. **Press the Home button.** The Home screen appears.
2. **Tap Settings.** The Settings screen appears.
3. **Tap Bluetooth.** The Bluetooth screen appears.
4. **Tap the Bluetooth switch and move it to the Off position.**

Minimize interference on your wireless network

Because so many people use wireless networks and wireless devices these days, it's easy to run into interference. This can slow down your wireless network and cause problems with time-sensitive technologies, such as AirPlay.

If your wireless network seems to be suffering from interference, you can look at the wireless channels that nearby networks are using and then switch your network to a channel that's either not in use or not being used much.

In Windows, you can use a third-party tool, such as inSSIDer (www.metageek.net/products/inssider) or NetStumbler (www.netstumbler.com/downloads), to see which wireless channels nearby networks are using. Both inSSIDer (shown in Figure 12.21) and NetStumbler are free.

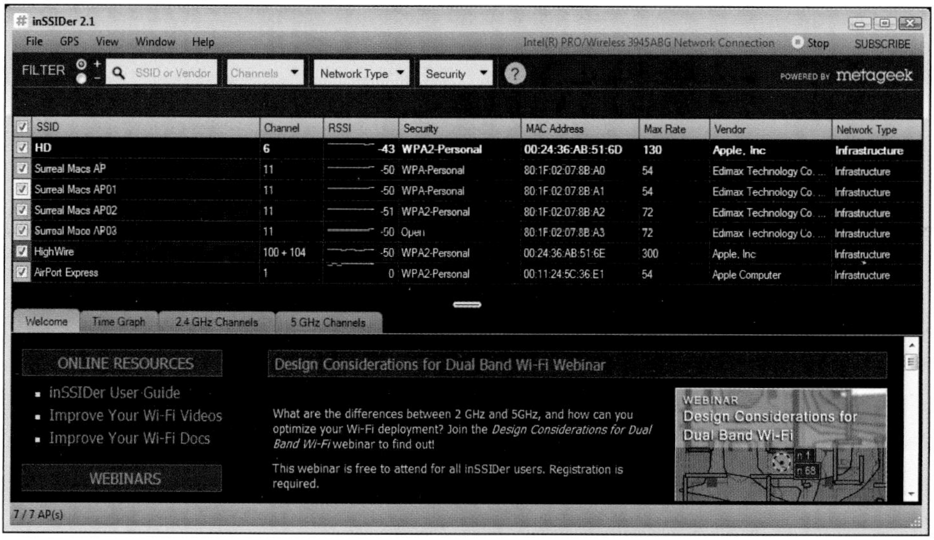

12.21 On a PC, you can use inSSIDer to find out which channels nearby wireless networks are using.

On OS X 10.8 (Mountain Lion), you can follow these steps to use the built-in Wi-Fi Diagnostics tool to analyze which wireless channels nearby networks are using:

1. **Option+click the Wi-Fi icon on the menu bar.** The Wi-Fi menu opens, showing its full set of options (because you held down Option), as shown in Figure 12.22.

2. **Click Open Wi-Fi Diagnostics.** The Wi-Fi Diagnostics window opens.

3. **Choose File ⇨ Network Utilities.** Alternatively, press ⌘+N. The Network Utilities window opens.

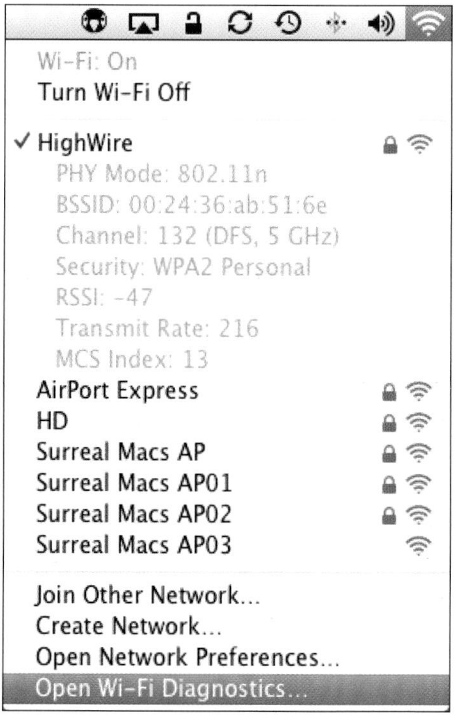

12.22 When you Option+click the Wi-Fi icon, the Wi-Fi menu includes the Open Wi-Fi Diagnostics command.

4. **Click Wi-Fi Scan in the toolbar.** The Wi-Fi Scan screen appears, as shown in Figure 12.23.

Network Name	BSSID	Channel ▲	Width	Band ▲	Security	Signal	Noise	Protocols	CC
AirPort Express	0:11:24:5c:36:e1	1	20 MHz	2.4 GHz	WPA2	-38	-92	b/g	
HD	0:24:36:ab:51:6d	6	20 MHz	2.4 GHz	WPA2	-29	-92	b/g/n	GB
Surreal Macs AP	80:1f:2:7:8b:a0	11	20 MHz	2.4 GHz	WPA	-43	-92	b/g	
Surreal Macs AP01	80:1f:2:7:8b:a1	11	20 MHz	2.4 GHz	WPA	-45	-92	b/g	
Surreal Macs AP03	80:1f:2:7:8b:a3	11	20 MHz	2.4 GHz	Open	-43	-92	b/g/n	
Surreal Macs AP02	80:1f:2:7:8b:a2	11	20 MHz	2.4 GHz	WPA2	-42	-92	b/g/n	
HighWire	0:24:36:ab:51:6e	100+1	20/40 MHz	5 GHz	WPA2	-38	-92	a/n	GB

Found 7 radios in 0.0 seconds · Scan

12.23 You can use the Wi-Fi Scan feature in Network Utilities to see which channels nearby wireless networks are using.

5. **If Wi-Fi Scan doesn't automatically scan the area for wireless networks and show the results, open the Scan pop-up menu in the lower-right corner and click Active Scan.**

6. **Click the Channel column heading to sort the scan results by channel.** You can then easily see which channels are the busiest and which are unused.

7. **Choose Wi-Fi Diagnostics ➪ Quit Wi-Fi Diagnostics.** The Network Utilities and Wi-Fi Diagnostics windows close.

After scanning your network, go into your wireless router's configuration screens and change the channel to one that is unused or less busy. How you change the channel depends on your wireless router, but the following example uses Apple's AirPort Extreme, which is a popular model:

1. **Click the Launchpad icon on the Dock.** The Launchpad screen appears.

2. **Type *air* to restrict the display to only items that include those letters.**

3. **Click AirPort Utility.** AirPort Utility opens and displays its initial screen.

4. **Click the AirPort that you want to configure.** The Information window opens, as
   shown in Figure 12.24.

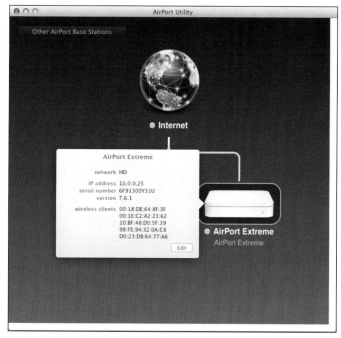

12.24 Click the AirPort that you want to configure to open its information
window.

5. **Click Edit.** The control screens for the
   AirPort appear.

6. **Click Wireless in the tab bar.** The
   Wireless tab appears, as shown in
   Figure 12.25.

12.25 On the AirPort Utility control screen, click
the Wireless tab.

7. **Click Wireless Options.** The Wireless Options dialog appears, as shown in Figure 12.26.

AirPort Utility

Wireless Options

☑ 5GHz network name: | HD 5GHz |

Country: | Finland ⬍ |

☐ Create hidden network

Radio Mode: | 802.11a/n – 802.11b/g/n (Automatic) ⬍ |

2.4GHz Channel: | 3 ⬍ |

5GHz Channel: | Automatic ⬍ |

[Cancel] [**Save**]

12.26 You can set the wireless channel in the Wireless Options dialog.

8. **Open the 2.4GHz Channel pop-up menu, and then choose the channel to use for your 2.4GHz network.**

9. **If you're using the 5GHz network too, open the 5GHz Channel pop-up menu, and then choose the channel to use.**

10. **Click Save.** The Wireless Options dialog closes.

11. **Click Update.** AirPort Utility displays a dialog warning that the device and its network services will be temporarily unavailable during the update, as shown in Figure 12.27.

12. **Click Continue.** AirPort Utility updates the AirPort Extreme. After the AirPort restarts, your wireless network uses the channel that you chose.

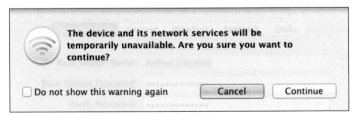

The device and its network services will be temporarily unavailable. Are you sure you want to continue?

☐ Do not show this warning again   [Cancel] [Continue]

12.27 This warning dialog appears before you update your network.

Setting your router to give AirPlay higher Quality of Service priority

Depending on the options your router offers, you may be able to set it to give AirPlay higher priority on your network. Higher priority can help AirPlay avoid skips and stutters, so if you're still having playback problems, it's worth spending a few minutes looking into your router's Quality of Service (QoS) settings.

Note Quality of Service (QoS) is a tool for telling your router how to prioritize the services, computers, and devices on your network. For example, many routers give priority to audio and video streams, because these are time-sensitive — delays to part of the stream can interrupt playback. By contrast, e-mail isn't time-sensitive and typically gets lower priority.

The settings that you need depend on your router, so you might have to do some sleuthing. In general, the following are the two main approaches:

- **Give AirPlay higher QoS.** If your router enables you to assign different priorities to services, crank up the priority for AirPlay.

- **Give your AirPlay devices higher QoS.** If your router doesn't let you change priorities for services, see if there's an option for giving devices higher QoS. You normally have to assign priorities by the MAC address, which is the hardware address of the network card (see the sidebar about finding MAC addresses for more details), not by the names or IP addresses of the computers or devices. Assign a lower priority to your network devices that don't use AirPlay, such as your printer.

Genius If you can choose whether to give higher QoS to AirPlay service or AirPlay devices, go with the service. The disadvantage to giving your AirPlay devices higher QoS is that they get precedence for everything they're doing — including e-mail, web surfing, or other low-priority activities — rather than just for AirPlay.

Finding the MAC Addresses of Your Computers and Devices

If you decide to implement Quality of Service (QoS) on your network to improve AirPlay, you may need to find the MAC addresses of your computers and devices. The MAC address is the Media Access Control address, the unique identifier of a network adapter. Each network adapter has its own unique MAC address. A MAC address is written in hexadecimal, base-16 counting that uses the numbers 0–9 and the letters A–F — for example, 98:FF:95:32:0A:C9.

Here's how to find the MAC addresses of your computers and devices:

- **Mac.** Choose Apple ⟹ System Preferences, and then click Network. In the Network preferences pane, click Ethernet or Wi-Fi (as needed), and then click Advanced. In the Advanced dialog, click Hardware, and then look at the MAC Address readout.

- **PC.** Choose Start ⟹ Control Panel. Click Network and Internet, and then click Network And Sharing Center. On the left side of the window, click Change Adapter Settings. Right-click the appropriate connection, and then click Properties. In the Properties dialog box, hold your mouse pointer over the Connect Using box. A ScreenTip appears showing the MAC address.

- **iPhone, iPod touch, or iPad.** From the Home screen, choose Settings ⟹ General ⟹ About, and then look at the Wi-Fi Address readout.

- **Apple TV.** From the Home screen, choose Settings ⟹ General ⟹ About, and then look at the Wi-Fi Address readout.

Configuring an Apple TV Using Apple Configurator

If you need to set up a lot of Apple TVs, you can automate the setup by using Apple Configurator. This is a free tool that Apple provides for configuring iOS devices — the iPhone, the iPod touch, the iPad, and the Apple TV. At this writing, Apple Configurator runs only on OS X, so you'll need a Mac to use it.

To use Apple Configurator, you create a file called a *configuration profile* containing the settings you want to apply. A configuration profile can contain different categories of settings, such as Wi-Fi settings or Restrictions settings. When you choose settings for a category, you are creating a *payload* for it.

Genius

Apple Configurator is designed to help you set up a slew of iOS devices quickly by automating the setup process. You may also want to use Apple Configurator if you need to make a single Apple TV use a proxy server because the Apple TV user interface doesn't offer this setting. To do so, you create a Wi-Fi payload in the configuration profile.

Getting started with Apple Configurator

Follow these steps to download and install Apple Configurator on your Mac:

1. **Click App Store on the Dock.** The App Store window opens.

2. **Click in the Search box in the upper-right corner.**

3. **Type *configurator*.** A list of search results appears.

4. **Click the Apple Configurator search result.** The Search Results screen appears.

5. **Click the Free button.** The Install App button appears.

6. **Click Install App.** Your Mac downloads Apple Configurator and installs it.

You can now launch Apple Configurator by clicking the Launchpad icon on the Dock and then clicking the Apple Configurator icon on the Launchpad screen. The first time that you run Apple Configurator, you must accept the license agreement. After you do so, the Apple Configurator opening screen appears, as shown in Figure 12.28. From this screen, you can prepare devices, and supervise and assign them.

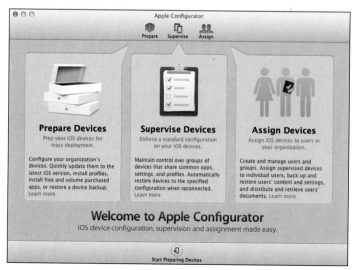

12.28 The Apple Configurator's opening screen.

Creating a configuration profile

Follow these steps to create a configuration profile with Apple Configurator:

1. **Click Prepare on the toolbar.** The Prepare pane appears.

2. **Click Add (+) in the lower-left corner.** The Add pop-up menu opens, as shown in Figure 12.29.

3. **Click Create New Profile.** The General pane appears.

4. **Click in the Name box shown in Figure 12.30, and then type a name for the configuration profile.** This enables you to identify the profile.

5. **Optionally, you can add information to the Organization and Description boxes.**

	Settings Apps
Name:	No Change
	☐ Number sequentially starting at 1
Supervision:	OFF
	Supervised devices can only be configured by Apple Configurator on this Mac.
iOS:	No Change
	☐ Erase before installing
Restore:	Don't Restore Backup
Profiles:	No Profiles Click + to add a profile
	+ − ⬀
	Import Profile...
	Create New Profile...

12.29 In the Prepare pane, click Add (+) at the bottom to open the pop-up menu.

12.30 In the General pane, type a name for the configuration profile.

6. **In the left pane, click the item that you want to configure, click the Configure button, and then choose settings.** The following actions create a Wi-Fi payload for connecting through a proxy server:

- **Click Wi-Fi.** The Wi-Fi pane appears, showing only a Configure button at first, as shown in Figure 12.31.

- **Click Configure.** The Wi-Fi pane displays the configuration controls, as shown in Figure 12.32.

- **Click in the Service Set Identifier (SSID) box, and then type the SSID (the network name) for the wireless network.**

12.31 The Wi-Fi pane appears with a Configure button.

- **Select the Hidden Network check box if the network is closed (that is, it doesn't broadcast its SSID).**

- **Select the Auto Join check box if you want the Apple TV to join this wireless network automatically.**

- **Open the Proxy Setup pop-up menu and choose Automatic or Manual.** Choose Automatic for an automatic proxy setup from a URL and Manual when you are going to provide the proxy information.

12.32 Use the Wi-Fi controls to create a Wi-Fi payload.

- **Enter the details for the proxy server.** For automatic setup, click in the Proxy Server URL box, and then type the URL for the proxy server. For a manual setup, enter the information in the left and right boxes in the Server and Port area, and the Authentication and Password boxes.

- **Open the Security Type pop-up menu, and then choose the security type for the network, such as WPA/WPA2.**

- **Click in the Password box, and then type the password for the Wi-Fi network.**

7. **Click Save.** Apple Configurator saves the configuration profile, and it appears in the Profiles list in the Prepare pane.

Installing a configuration profile on an Apple TV

When you have created a configuration profile for the Apple TV, you're ready to install it. If the Apple TV is new, you must perform the initial part of the setup manually. If you've already set up the Apple TV, and you're installing the configuration profile to change its configuration, you don't need to do this.

If you're setting up an Apple TV from scratch, follow these steps before installing the configuration profile:

1. **Connect the Apple TV to a TV or monitor using an HDMI cable.**

2. **Connect the Apple TV power cable.** The Apple TV powers on automatically and displays the Welcome to Apple TV screen.

3. **Highlight your language by pressing the Down or Up button on the Apple Remote, and then press the Select button to select the language.**

4. **Press the Menu button to skip configuring the network.**

Once your Apple TV is prepared, follow these steps to install the configuration profile:

1. **Unplug the power cable from the Apple TV.**

2. **Unplug the HDMI cable from the Apple TV's HDMI port.**

3. **Connect a micro-USB cable to the Apple TV's micro-USB port.**

4. **Connect the USB end of the cable to a USB port on your Mac.**

5. **Reconnect the power cable to the Apple TV.** The Apple TV starts. When your Mac detects the Apple TV, Apple Configurator opens.

Note If your Mac doesn't launch Apple Configurator automatically, click the Launchpad icon on the Dock, and then click the Apple Configurator icon to launch Apple Configurator manually.

6. **Click Prepare on the Apple Configurator toolbar.** The Prepare pane appears.

7. **In the Profiles list box, select the configuration profile that you want to apply.**

8. **Choose Devices ⇨ Apply.** The confirmation dialog shown in Figure 12.33 appears.

Are you sure you want to apply these settings to all USB-connected devices?

Choosing Apply will prepare all USB-connected devices with these settings and apps, including devices connected during the prepare process.

☐ Do not ask me again

Cancel   Apply

12.33 Click the Apply button to apply the selected configuration profile to the Apple TV.

9. **Click Apply.** Apple Configurator displays a dialog prompting you to install the configuration profile on the Apple TV.

10. **Click Install on the Apple TV.** Apple Configurator installs the configuration profile on the Apple TV.

11. **When the installation finishes, unplug the micro-USB cable from the Apple TV, and then reconnect the HDMI cable to the Apple TV.**

Index

A

AAC (Advanced Audio Coding), 63, 71
About screen, 225, 227
AC power cable, 4, 10, 13
Accessibility screen, 44
accessibility settings, 42, 44
Account Information screen, 95, 236
Account Name screen, 48, 56, 165
Activating screen, 16
adapter settings, 24
adapters, 5, 20, 252
Add Flickr Contact screen, 49, 171
Add To Library dialog, 70
Adding Files dialog (iTunes), 69–70
Advanced Audio Coding (AAC), 63, 71
Advanced dialog (Security & Privacy), 219
Advanced Preferences pane (iTunes), 64–65
AIFF (Audio Interchange File Format), 63, 71–72
Airfoil, 87
AirParrot, 202–206
AirParrot Driver Not Found dialog, 203
AirPlay
    finding unlisted podcasts, 154–155
    playing music stored on computer, 103
    playing unlisted radio station, 148–149
    setting up, 55
    streaming music, 86–88
    streaming screen of iOS device, 88–89
    troubleshooting, 241–252

AirPlay dialog, 88–89
AirPlay Mirroring, 87–88, 205
AirPlay screen, 55, 242
AirPort Express, 88, 103
AirPort Utility control screen, 250
Albums screen, 84
All Podcasts list, 151
All Songs screen, 84
analog speaker, 12
Any Video Converter Ultimate, 142
AnyDVD, 142
App icons, troubleshooting disappearance of, 231
Apple, option of sending information to, 17
Apple Configurator, 35, 252–257
Apple ID
    about, 92–93
    Home Sharing, 56, 60, 95–97, 233–237
    Movies app, 108
    signing in with, 45–46
    troubleshooting, 240
Apple Lossless Encoding, 62–63, 71–72
Arrangement pane (extending Mac desktop), 206
Artists screen, 83
attenuation, 12
aTV Flash, 207–209
Audio & Video screen, 51–53
Audio Interchange File Format (AIFF), 63, 71–72
Audio language screen, 52–53
Audio Output setting, 52
audio settings, 51–54

audio-only podcasts, 146
audio-visual standard, 5
authorization, 93–95, 235
Auto video output format, 53–54
AVI (movie format), 200

B

battery (remote control), 176, 220
Beamer app, 136, 200–201
bitrate, 63
Bluetooth, 246
Blu-ray, 54, 140
Button Already Learned screen, 181
Buy screen, 112–113, 118

C

cables
    AC power cable, 4, 10, 13
    converter cable, 5
    Ethernet cable, 4, 10, 13–14, 18, 246
    HDMI cable, 6–7, 10–11, 216, 230, 240, 257
    micro USB cable, 216, 257
    optical audio cable, 12
    optical digital audio port and cable, 10
    power cable, 4
    recommended length, 12
    TOSLINK cable, 12
    USB cable, 184, 233, 257
camera, digital, 136–137, 158
Camera Roll, 158
Categories screen, 129, 151
CD Info dialog, 66–67
CDs
    adding protected WMA files to iTunes, 72
    Compilation CD check box, 67
    compilations, 67, 84
    encoding, 63
    importing, 66–68
    setting iTunes to create high-quality
        audio files, 61–62
Change Current Destination Folder screen, 161
children, restricting access to, 37–40, 108, 127
Choose Photos screen, 47–49
Classic screen saver, 50, 168

CloneDVD, 142
CloneDVD mobile, 142
Closed Captioning, 52
Compilation CD check box, 67
compilations, 67, 84
Compilations screen, 84
Component Video, 5, 7–9, 11
Composer tag, 85
Composers list, 85
Composite Video, 5, 7–9, 11
Computers screen, 56–57, 101–102
Configuration Done! screen, 34
configuration profile, 252, 254–257
Configuration Succeeded screen, 19
Configure an internet-sharing network dialog, 22
Configure Wi-Fi, 15, 19, 227–228
Confirm Passcode screen, 39
connecting
    D-sub connector, 11
    to headphones, 12
    to the Internet, 13, 236–239
    Internet Connection Sharing (ICS), 13, 20–25
    to Internet through proxy server, 35
    to network, 14–17, 19, 226
    to power socket, 13
    to speakers, 12
    troubleshooting, 236–239
    TV or monitor, 11
    wireless network, 19
Connecting screen, 16
connection types, 9
content issues, troubleshooting, 239–241
Control screen, 186
converter adapter, 5
converter box, 9, 230
converter cable, 5
converter device, 11
converters
    Any Video Converter Ultimate, 142
    digital-to-analog (DAC) converter, 4, 12
    file converter, 137
    HDMI-to-Component Video converter, 8, 230
    HDMI-to-Composite Video converter, 8, 230
copyright, 140, 240–241
Cube transition, 50, 168

D

DAC (digital-to-analog) converter, 4, 12

DD-WRT, 35

deauthorization, of computers, 94–95, 235–236

Deauthorize This Computer dialog, 235

decryption utility, 142

Deep Color, 7

Default Music screen, 167

Details screen, 19

DHCP (Dynamic Host Configuration
    Protocol), 15, 18, 221, 223–224, 228

digital camera, 136–137, 158

digital rights management (DRM), 71, 240

digital video interface (DVI), 11

digital-to-analog (DAC) converter, 4, 12

display issues, troubleshooting, 230–232

Displays pane (extending the
    Mac desktop), 205–206

Dissolve transition, 50, 168

DNS (Domain Name Service)
    address, 31, 34–35, 221, 223–224, 228–229

Dolby TrueHD, 7

DRM (digital rights management), 71, 240

D-sub connector, 11

DVDs
    creating video files, 140–142
    encoding of video content, 54
    legalities of copying, 140
    SD DVDs, 140
    title, 138
    XBMC, 208

DVDSmith, Inc., 142

DVI (digital video interface), 11

Dynamic Host Configuration Protocol
    (DHCP), 15, 18, 221, 223–224, 228

E

EasyWMA, 72

encoding
    Apple Lossless Encoding, 62–63, 71–72
    CDs, 63
    FLAC (Free Lossless Audio Codec), 72
    Ogg Vorbis encoder, 72
    of video content, 54

encryption, 227

Energy Saver pane, 239

error connection, 63

Ethernet, connecting Apple TV via, 236

Ethernet cable, 4, 10, 13–14, 18, 246

Ethernet card, for setting PC to wake for
    network access, 238

Ethernet connection, for Internet
    Sharing, 20–21, 23, 25

Ethernet port, 10, 15, 20

Ethernet TCP/IP Setup, 32–35, 222–223

EuroAV, 9

Euroconnector, 9

EuroSCART, 9

Explorer window, 69

F

Featured Channels screen (Vimeo), 128–129

Featured Providers screen (podcasts), 152

file converter, 137

file-conversion utilities, 137

files, copying between computer libraries, 99

Final Cut, 136

Finder window, 69

FireCore, 207

Firewall screen, 241

FireWire, 21

fixed playlists, 72–73, 81

FLAC (Free Lossless Audio Codec) encoder, 72

Flickr photos
    adding contact, 170–171
    browsing contact's albums and viewing
        slide shows, 172–173
    for screen saver, 47–49
    searching contact, 171–172
    sharing, 169

Flickr screen, 170–172

Flickr Search screen, 172

Flip transition, 168

Floating screen saver, 47, 49

FLV (movie format), 200

Free Lossless Audio Codec (FLAC) encoder, 72

G

G rating, 40
Gapless Album check box, 67
GarageBand (podcast creator), 155
General pane, 219, 255
General Preferences pane (iTunes), 61, 66
General screen, 30–31, 212
general settings, configuration of, 42–46
Genius feature, 82, 114, 116
Genius information screen, 82
Genius Mixes, 82
Genius Playlist, 82, 86
Genius screen, 114
Genres lists, 114
Genres screen
    Hulu Plus, 122–123
    movies, 110
    music, 85
    Netflix, 122
    TV shows, 115–116
Great Documentaries, 109

H

H.264 (video format), 109, 134
HandBrake, 137–141
HandBrake Presets pane, 139
HD (high definition), 46, 109
HDCP (High-Bandwidth Digital
    Content Protection), 240–241
HDMI (High-Definition Multimedia Interface), 5, 9
HDMI 1.2, 7
HDMI 1.3, 7
HDMI cable, 6–7, 10–11, 216, 230, 240, 257
HDMI connection type, 9, 11
HDMI hub, 230
HDMI input, 7–8, 11, 230
HDMI output, 51, 53–54
HDMI Output screen, 53–54
HDMI port, 5, 10–11, 257
HDMI signal, 11
HDMI signal restorer, 7
HDMI standards, 7
HDMI-to-Component Video converter, 8, 230
HDMI-to-Composite Video converter, 8, 230

HDTV, 5–6, 11
headphones, 11–12
high definition (HD), 46, 109
High-Bandwidth Digital Content
    Protection (HDCP), 240–241
High-Definition Multimedia Interface (HDMI), 5, 9
Home folder, 64
Home screen
    app icons, 231
    displaying, 17
    Movies and TV Shows apps, 239
    navigating with, 14
Home Sharing
    copying files between
        computer libraries, 99–101
    deauthorizing computer, 95
    playing content on another computer, 98–99
    playing content on Apple TV, 101–102
    playing content on iOS device, 103–104
    playing content on iPad, 104–105
    playing music on Apple TV, 60
    restarting, 237
    sending movies to Apple TV, 200–201
    setting up in iTunes, 92–95
    setting up on Apple TV, 97–98
    setting up on iOS device, 96–97
    troubleshooting, 232–239
    turning on, 56–57, 184–186
    understanding, 92
Home Sharing Is On screen, 57, 98
Home Sharing screen, 93–94, 97, 184–185, 237
Home Sharing Settings dialog, 101
Home Sharing Setup screen, 56, 97, 98
Hulu, 124
Hulu Plus, 108, 123–127

I

iCloud, playing music, 60, 77–86
iCloud account, 158
iCloud Control Panel, 160–163
iCloud dialog, 162
iCloud Photo Stream. *See* Photo Stream
iCloud Preferences pane, 159
ICS (Internet Connection Sharing), 13, 20–25

iLife, 136

iMovie, 136–137, 155, 220

Import Settings dialog, 62

Information dialog (song), 67–68

inSSIDer, 246–247

Installation Options screen, 160–161

Internet connection

  checking, 234

  choosing suitable video resolution for, 232

  connecting Apple TV to Internet, 13

  lack of speed, 45–46

  sharing with Apple TV, 13, 20–25

  switching from one wireless network to
    another, 18–20

  through proxy server, 35

Internet Connection Sharing (ICS), 13, 20–25

Internet issues, troubleshooting, 228–232

Internet photos, 39

Internet Protocol (IP), 31, 221

Internet Protocol version 4 (IPv4), 221

Internet Protocol version 6 (IPv6), 221

Internet radio, 37, 39, 146–149, 208

Internet Service Provider (ISP), 34

Internet Sharing, 13, 20–21

iOS devices. *See also* iPad; iPhone; iPod touch

  AirPlay, 87–89

  creating video, 136

  downloading/installing Remote app
    using, 183–184

  Home Sharing, 60, 103–104

  Photo Stream, 164

  playing content, 103–104

  as remote control, 183

  screen of to Apple TV, 88–89

  streaming music, 60, 87–88

IP (Internet Protocol), 31, 221

IP address, 15, 18, 33, 221

iPad

  AirPlay, 85, 242, 246

  AirPlay Mirroring, 88

  Apple Configurator, 252

  Apple ID, 220

  camera, 220

  confirmation dialog, 217

  downloading/installing Remote app, 183–184

  Home Sharing, 60, 96, 104–105

  interface, 184

  setting up Photo Stream, 164

  as source of photos, 158

  streaming music, 60, 87–88

  streaming screen of to Apple TV, 88–89

iPad Apps list, 183

iPhone

  AirPlay, 242, 246

  AirPlay Mirroring, 88

  Apple Configurator, 252

  Apple ID, 220

  camera, 220

  confirmation dialog, 217

  downloading/installing Remote app, 183–184

  Home Sharing, 60

  playing content via Home Sharing, 103–104

  setting up Home Sharing, 96–97

  setting up Photo Stream, 164

  as source of photos, 158

  streaming music, 60, 87–88

  streaming screen of to Apple TV, 88–89

iPhone Apps list, 183

iPod touch

  AirPlay, 242

  AirPlay Mirroring, 88

  Apple Configurator, 252

  Apple ID, 220

  camera, 220

  confirmation dialog, 217

  downloading/installing Remote app, 183–184

  Home Sharing, 60

  interface, 184

  playing content via Home Sharing, 103–104

  setting up Home Sharing, 96–97

  setting up Photo Stream, 164

  as source of photos, 158

  streaming music, 60, 87–88

  streaming screen of to Apple TV, 88–89

IPv4 (Internet Protocol version 4), 221

IPv6 (Internet Protocol version 6), 221

ISP (Internet Service Provider), 34

iTunes

  accepting video files, 134–135

  adding existing music files, 69–70

Adding Files dialog, 69
adding video file, 134–136
Advanced Audio Coding (AAC), 63
Advanced Preferences pane, 64–65
AIFF (Audio Interchange File Format), 63, 71
AirPlay, 86–87, 242
Apple Lossless Encoding, 63
Composer tag, 85
confirmation dialog, 217
controlling quality of music, 62
copying of files from one computer library
    to another, 99–101
creating files from CDs, 61–62
downloading movies, 112
downloading TV shows, 118
downloading/installing Remote app, 183–184
encoding, 62–63
General Preferences pane, 61, 66
Home Sharing, 52, 56, 92–95, 200
importing CDs, 66–68
importing music files, 71
importing video from DVDs, 140
Keep iTunes Media folder organized
    check box, 64
movie formats, 200
MPEG-4 movie files, 134
opening podcasts, 154–155
playing content on computer, 98
playing music, 60
playing unlisted radio station, 148–149
playlists, 73–77
Publish your project to iTunes dialog, 136–137
QuickTime, 134
restarting, 236
running on Mac, 61
Search iTunes Movies screen, 113
Search iTunes Store Podcasts screen, 152
Search iTunes Store TV Shows screen, 117
unable to play content, 239
updating to latest version, 233
WAV (Waveform Audio File Format), 63, 71
WMA (Windows Media Audio), 71–72
WMV (movie format), 137
X Lossless Decoder (XLD), 72
iTunes libraries, 56, 60, 64–66, 92,
    99, 137, 155, 236

iTunes Match
    cost of, 77
    parental controls, 37, 39
    playing music, 60
    setting up, 77–79
iTunes Media folder, 65
iTunes Media library, 92
iTunes Store
    account configuration, 45–46
    Account screen, 36, 46
    compilations, 84
    Location screen, 239
    message that is unavailable, 224, 228–229
    Password screen, 36, 46
    protected video content, 134
    reducing resolution, 232
    screen, 45–46
    unable to play content, 241

J
jailbreaking, 206–207
Just for Kids screen, 122

K
Ken Burns screen saver, 50, 168
keyboard, on-screen, 16–17, 208

L
language option, 14
Language screen, 44
language setting, 44, 52–53, 257
Launchpad screen, 92, 138, 200–201, 248
Learn Remote screen, 178–180
License Agreement screen, 160
Lion, 202
The Little App Factory, 141
Location screen (iTunes Store), 239
Lossless Encoding, 62–63, 71–72

M
M4V extension, 134
Mac
    AAC and MP3 files, 72
    Add to Library, 70
    Airfoil, 87

Mac *(continued)*

AirParrot, 202–203, 205

Apple Configurator, 35, 252–253, 257

Beamer app, 136, 200–201

checking remote battery, 220

configuration profile, 257

copying URLs, 148, 154

creating podcasts, 155

creating video files from video clips, 136

EasyWMA, 72

editing Smart playlist, 73, 76

Energy Saver pane, 239

extending desktop to Apple TV, 205–206

Finder window, 69

finding MAC addresses, 252

GarageBand (podcast creator), 155

iMovie, 136, 155

importing photos, 158

importing video, 136

installing HandBrake, 138

Internet Sharing, 13, 20–21

launching iTunes, 92

Lion, 202

Mountain Lion, 202, 205

Open (iTunes library), 70

opening Smart Playlist dialog, 74

Preferences dialog, 61–62, 64–65

restarting computer, 237

restarting Home Sharing, 237

restarting iTunes, 236

RipIt, 141

running of iTunes, 61

Safari, 234

selecting on, 100

setting up Photo Stream, 158–160

Snow Leopard, 202

software updates, 233, 243

troubleshooting remote control, 218–219

turning on wake for network
     access feature, 237–239

/Users/Shared/folder, 65

VLC video player, 138

MAC (Media Access Control)
     address, 20, 245, 252

media files, sharing of, 65

Menu button, 14

micro USB cable, 216, 257

micro USB port, 10, 216, 257

mirroring, computer on Apple TV
     with AirParrot, 202–206

monitor, 9, 11, 54, 70, 205–206, 241, 257

More panel (Home Sharing), 104, 105

More screen, 103, 111

Motion JPEG (video format), 134

Mountain Lion, 202, 205, 247

MOV extension, 134

movie formats, 137, 200

movies

buying, 112–113

Genius recommendations, 114

previewing and renting, 112

Purchased List, 114

searching and finding, 113

sending to Apple TV, 200–201

Wish List, 114

Movies App, 108, 109–114, 239

Movies screen, 109–110, 113–114, 126

MP3 Encoder dialog, 62

MP3 format, 62–63, 71–72

MP4 extension, 134

MPEG-4 (video format), 134

Multiple Speakers dialog, 87

music. *See also* iTunes

playing, 60, 98–99

streaming, 86–88

music file formats, converting, 71–72

music library, 60–65. *See also* iTunes libraries

Music Playlists screen, 81

Music screen, 96–97, 103–104

Music Videos screen, 81

My Watch Later screen (Vimeo), 130

N

Name screen, 30–31

naming (Apple TV), 30–31

Navigation pane (NETGEAR), 245

Netflix

Ask setting, 39

Netflix app, 108

parental controls, 37
   selecting movies and shows, 121–122
   viewing information about/watching, 123
NETGEAR router, 245
NetStumbler, 246
network adapter, 238, 252
Network and Sharing Center window, 24
network configuration, 31–34, 36–37
Network Connections screen, 24
network issues, troubleshooting, 220–227
Network preferences pane (MAC addresses), 252
network problems, 31
Network screen, 18–19, 31–32, 34, 222, 225–229
network settings, 221–224
Network Setup screen, 32, 222, 228
Network Test, 36–37, 229
Network Utilities screen, 248
New & Noteworthy
   Movies app, 109–110
   podcasts, 150–151
   TV shows, 116
New Releases screen, 122
Now Displaying screen, 54
Now Playing screen, 82

O

Ogg Vorbis encoder, 72
1080p resolution, 45, 109, 127, 134, 232
on-screen keyboard, 16–17, 208
Open Stream dialog, 149
optical audio cable, 12
optical audio connection, 5
optical digital audio port and cable, 10
Origami screen saver, 47, 49
OS X
   AirParrot, 202–203
   Apple Configurator, 252
   creating files from video clips, 136
   finding name of wireless network, 244
   Mountain Lion, 202, 205, 247
   tools for copying DVD files, 140–141
OS X Internet Sharing, 20, 22
OS X Launchpad screen, 138

P

pairing the remote, 41, 218
parental controls, 37–40, 109, 127
passcode, 37–40
password, 13, 16, 46, 55, 92–93, 227
Password screen, 165
payload, 252
PC
   Add Folder to Library, 70
   AirParrot, 202–204
   CD dialog box, 66–67
   checking remote battery, 220
   copying URLs, 148, 154
   creating podcasts, 155
   editing Smart playlist, 73, 76
   Explorer window, 69
   finding MAC addresses, 252
   importing photos, 158
   importing video, 136
   installing HandBrake, 138
   iTunes dialog box, 61–62, 64–65
   iTunes track naming, 64
   Public Music window, 65
   red-green-blue encoding, 54
   restarting computer, 237
   restarting Home Sharing, 237
   restarting iTunes, 236
   revealing name of wireless network, 244
   Select Folder (iTunes library), 70
   selecting noncontiguous items, 100
   setting to wake for network access, 238
   setting up Photo Stream, 160–163
   software updates, 243
   using inSSIDer, 247
   WAV (Waveform Audio File Format), 71–72
Péritel, 9
PG rating, 40
PG-13 rating, 40
Photo Stream
   browsing individual photos, 166–168
   choosing slide show settings, 167–168
   deleting photos, 169

Photo Stream *(continued)*
   screen savers, 47–48
   setting up on Apple TV, 164
   setting up on iOS device, 164
   setting up on Mac, 158–160
   setting up on PC, 160–163
   understanding, 158
   viewing photos with, 166–169
   viewing slide show, 167
Photo Stream Options dialog, 160, 163
Photo Stream screen, 166–167, 169
Photo Stream Setup screen, 48, 164–165
Photos & Cameras screen, 164
Pixar Classics, 109
plasma screen, 47
playlists, 72–77, 81
Play/Pause button, 14
podcasts
   finding, 150–155
   making your own, 155
   parental controls, 37–39
   viewing information about/playing, 153–154
Podcasts screen, 150–152
Popular and Recommended screen, 125
ports
   Ethernet port, 10, 15, 20
   HDMI port, 5, 10–11, 257
   micro USB port, 10, 216, 257
   optical digital audio port and cable, 10
   power port/connector, 10
   USB port, 216, 257
power cable, 4
power port/connector, 10
power supply, 4, 9, 13
Prepare pane (configuration profile), 254, 256–257
Presets pane (HandBrake), 139
Properties dialog, 24–25
proxy server, 35
Public Music window, 65
Purchased screen, 114, 119

Q
QoS Setup screen, 245
Quality of Services (QoS), 245, 251
QuickTime, 134

R
R rating, 40
radio, Internet. *See* Internet radio
Radio and Television Receiver
   Manufacturers' Association, 5
Radio app, 146–149
Radio screen, 146, 148
Remote app, 183–186
remote control
   choosing, 177
   configuration, 177–181
   described, 4
   navigation, 14
   pairing, 41
   renaming, reconfiguring,
     or deleting, 181–182
   replacing battery, 176
   third-party, 178
   troubleshooting, 218–220
   using iOS device as, 183
Remote Control Name screen, 178–179, 182
Remote screen, 185
Remotes screen, 41, 177, 181
Rent screen, 112
rented movies, 112
Reset, 213–216
resolution, 54, 232. *See also* 720p resolution;
   1080p resolution
Restart, 213–214
Restore, 213, 215
restriction ratings, 40
RGB High video output format, 54
RGB Low video output format, 54
Riplt, 141
Rogue Amoeba Software LLC, 87
router
   connection speed, 231
   connections, 13
   DHCP (Dynamic Host Configuration
     Protocol), 15
   network settings, 223–228
   troubleshooting, 236, 241, 243–245, 248, 251
router address, 34, 221, 223–224

S

Save Movie panel (video clips), 137
SCART (Syndicat des Constructeurs d'Appareils Radiorécepteurs et Téléviseurs), 5, 9
Schedule screen (WSJ Live), 190
screen saver, 47–51, 165–166, 168
Screen Saver screen, 47, 49–50, 168
ScreenTip, 244
SD DVDs, 140
Search iTunes Store Movies screen, 113
Search iTunes Store Podcasts screen, 152
Search iTunes Store TV Shows screen, 117
Search screen
    Hulu Plus, 126
    iOS devices, 183
    iTunes Match, 80–81
    movies, 114
    Netflix, 122
    Vimeo, 130
    WSJ Live, 196–197
Security & Privacy pane (remote control), 219
Select button, 14
selecting (choosing an item), 14
Set Passcode screen, 38–39
setting up
    choosing whether to send information to Apple, 17
    connecting Apple TV to network, 14–15
    starting Apple TV and choosing language, 14
Settings screen, 30–31
Setup Complete screen (remote), 180
720p resolution, 45, 109, 134, 232
Shared panel (Home Sharing), 104–105
Shared screen, 103–104
Show setting (importing a CD), 66
sleep, 26
slide show
    Flickr, 173
    Photo Stream, 167–168
SlySoft, 142
Smart Playlist dialog, 75–76
Smart playlists, 72–77, 81
Snow Leopard, 202
software updates, 212–213

Songs screen, 84
Sound Check, 51–52
Source list (iTunes library), 69
speakers, 4, 9–12, 87–88, 103
Speedtest.net, 231
standard TV, 7–8, 11, 54
status light, 14, 213–214, 216, 219, 230
streaming
    of iOS device screen to Apple TV, 88–89
    music from iCloud, 13
    music from iOS device, 60, 87–88
    music from Mac or PC, 86
    Network Test, 36
    screen of iOS devices to Apple TV, 88–89
    videos, 13, 36, 45, 225
StrongVPN, 35
subnet mask, 31, 33, 221, 223–224, 228
Subscribe to Podcast dialog, 155
Subtitle Language screen, 52
subtitles, 52, 178
Summary screen
    iOS devices, 233
    WSJ Live, 192–193, 196–197
surge protector, 13
Syndicat des Constructeurs d'Appareils Radiorécepteurs et Téléviseurs (SCART), 5, 9

T

TCP/IP (Transmission Control Protocol/Internet Protocol)
    addressing, 221
    Ethernet, 32–35, 222–223
    settings, 33
    Wi-Fi, 32
time zone setting, 42–43
title (on DVD), 138
Top Movies screen, 109
Top Podcasts screen, 150–151
Toshiba Link, 10
TOSLINK cable, 12
TOSLINK connector, 10
trailers, 39
Trailers App, 108, 119–120

Trailers screen, 126
transitions (for screen saver), 50, 168
troubleshooting
    AirPlay, 241–252
    content issues, 239–241
    essential troubleshooting moves, 213–217
    Home Sharing, 232–239
    Internet connection issues, 228–229
    network issues, 220–227
    remote control issues, 218–220
TV Networks & Studios screen, 115
TV Resolution screen, 54
TV screen, 125
TV shows
    browsing and finding, 115
    returning to previously purchased, 119
    viewing show info and finding
        episodes, 117–118
    watching previews and adding
        to Favorites, 118–119
TV Shows App, 108, 114–119, 239
TV Shows screen, 114–117, 119, 122
TV-14 rating, 40
TV-G rating, 40
TV-MA rating, 40
TV-PG rating, 40
TV-Y rating, 40
TV-Y7 rating, 40
21-pin connector, 5

U
unboxing, 4
Up, Down, Left, and Right buttons, 14
Update screen, 243
updating, 212–213
USB cable, 184, 233, 257
USB cable, micro, 216, 257
USB connector, 21, 216
USB port, 216, 257
USB port, micro, 10, 157, 216
Use Photo Stream as Screen Saver screen, 165
User Account Control dialog, 161
Users & Groups pane (AirParrot), 202

V
VGA, 11
video
    creating with iOS device, 136
    formats, 109, 134, 137–139
    output format, 53–54
    playing via Home Sharing, 98–99
    resolution, 232
    settings, 51–54
    streaming, 13, 36, 45, 225
    watching on Hulu Plus, 127
    watching on Vimeo, 127
video files
    creating from DVDs, 140–142
    creating from video clips, 136–137
Videos app, 104
Videos by Category (WSJ Live), 194–195
Vimeo, 127–131
Vimeo Categories screen, 129
Vimeo Featured Channels screen, 128–129
Vimeo home screen, 128
vimeo items, 39
VLC video player, 138, 140
VoiceOver, 43

W
wake for network access, 237–239
Wall Street Journal, 190
walled garden, 207
WAV (Waveform Audio File Format), 71
WAV encoder, 63
websites
    AirParrot, 202
    Apple iCloud, 160
    Apple Store, 176
    Beamer, 200
    DD-WRT, 35
    Digital Content Protection, 241
    DVDSmith, Inc., 142
    EasyWMA, 72
    FireCore, LLC, 207
    HandBrake, 138
    Hulu, 124
    inSSIDer, 246

The Little App Factory, 141
NetStumbler, 246
Rogue Amoeba Software LLC, 87
SlySoft, 142
Speedtest.net, 231
StrongVPN, 35
Vimeo, 127
VLC video player, 140
X Lossless Decoder (XLD), 72
xACT, 72
Welcome to Apple TV screen, 14
Welcome to iCloud screen, 161
What's Hot (podcasts), 151
When you insert a CD pop-up menu, 66
Wi-Fi adapter, 20
Wi-Fi address, 20
Wi-Fi Ethernet Setup, 32–34
Wi-Fi Network screen, 15, 16, 19, 227
Wi-Fi pane (configuration profile), 255
Wi-Fi password, 227
Wi-Fi Password screen, 16–17, 19
Wi-Fi payload, 256
Wi-Fi Scan feature, 248
Wi-Fi screen, 243
Wi-Fi TCP/IP Setup, 32
Wi-Fi TCP/IP Setup screen, 229
Windows
    AirParrot, 203–204
    creating files from video clips, 32
    creating movies, 136
    Internet Connection
        Sharing (ICS), 13, 20, 23–25
    Internet Explorer, 234
    iTunes, 61, 71, 92
    launching iTunes, 92
    minimizing interference on
        wireless network, 246
    Rogue Amoeba Software LLC, 87
    tools for copying DVD files, 142
Windows Live Movie Maker, 155
Windows Media Audio (WMA) format, 71–72
Windows Media Player, 71–72
Windows movie Maker, 155
Windows notification area, 204
Windows Security Alert dialog, 204

wired network
    advantage of, 13, 246
    changing from or to, 18
    connecting Apple TV, 9–10, 13
    manually configuring Apple TV
        network settings, 221
    troubleshooting connection issues, 224
    troubleshooting Home Sharing issues, 234
wireless network
    changing from or to, 18
    disadvantage of, 13, 246
    manually configuring Apple TV
        network settings, 221
    minimizing interference on, 246
    selection of, 15–16
    troubleshooting connection issues, 225–228
    troubleshooting Home Sharing issues, 234
Wireless Options dialog, 250
Wizard screens, AirParrot Setup, 203–204
WMA (Windows Media Audio) format, 71–72
WMV (movie format), 200
WPA Enterprise encryption, 227
WPA2 Enterprise encryption, 227
WSJ Live App
    browsing by category, 194–195
    browsing full list, 192–193
    browsing schedule, 190–192
    finding programs, 190–197
    opening, 190
    searching for programs, 196–197
    watching live broadcasts, 190
WSJ Live home screen, 190, 194, 196
WSJ Live screen, 190

X

X Lossless Decoder (XLD), 72
xACT, 72
XBMC Media Center, 208

Y

YCbCr video output format, 54
Yesterday Schedule screen (WSJ Live), 191
YouTube, 37, 39